NEW AND

Giulio

Southampton, 2025

JULIAN STANNARD has published nine collections of poetry; the most recent being *Please Don't Bomb the Ghost of My Brother* (Salt, 2023). His work has been nominated for Forward (UK) and Pushcart Prizes (USA). He has been awarded the George Crabbe Memorial Poetry Prize, the International Troubadour Prize for Poetry and the Lerici Shelley Prize for Poetry. *Sottoripa: Genoese Poems*, a bilingual publication, was brought out by Canneto in 2018. For many years he taught at the University of Genoa. He has written several monographs including *Fleur Adcock in Context: From Movement to Martians* (Edwin Mellen Press, 1997) and *Basil Bunting* (Liverpool University Press, 2014) The American publisher Sagging Meniscus Press brought out a novel, *The University Of Bliss*, in 2024.

Rina's War (Peterloo Poets, 2001)

The Red Zone (Peterloo Poets, 2007)

The Parrots of Villa Gruber Discover Lapis Lazuli (Salmon Poetry, 2011)

The Street of Perfect Love (Worple Press, 2014)

What were you thinking? (CB Editions, 2016)

Sottoripa: Genoese Poems (Canneto Editore, 2018)

Average is the New Fantastico (Green Bottle Press, 2019)

Heat Wave (Salt, 2020)

Please Don't Bomb the Ghost of My Brother (Salt, 2023)

Julian Stannard

New Selected Poems

SALT

CROMER

PUBLISHED BY SALT PUBLISHING 2025

2 4 6 8 10 9 7 5 3 1

First published in Great Britain in 2025 by
Salt Publishing Ltd
12 Norwich Road, Cromer, NR27 0AX United Kingdom
www.saltpublishing.com

Salt Publishing Limited Reg. No. 5293401

A CIP catalogue record for this book is available from the British Library

ISBN 978 1 78463 338 7 (Paperback edition)

Typeset in Sabon by Salt Publishing

Printed and bound in Great Britain by Clays Ltd, Elcograf S.p.A

This book is for Jack and William

Contents

New Poems

The Pool

The chief leaf man rises early.
A breeze in the banyan tree.
The water laps.
Skink lizard on the prowl.

Perfection. Blue. Perfection.
No leaves on the water.
Miles Davis – his ghost –
becoming the banyan tree.

Chief leaf man sees a leaf
in the corner of the pool
and shouts in Vietnamese.
Leaf man number two crouches,
picks it out.

The apprentice leaf boy,
conical hat,
takes a broom from the storeroom.
Sweeps.

The hotel dog – a Saigon mongrel – watches.

Eternal – mythological – war of leaves.
The frangipani quickens.

I watch its petals drop upon the water.

A stiffening breeze from Saigon River.
The palm trees writhe and thrash.

Tung Street
Hong Kong

It's the saloon
at the end
of the typhoon.

It's Tung Street.
Cannonball street.
Tongue-lashed street.

The Battle of Dien Bien Phu.
The Siege of Mafeking.
The Boxer Rebellion.
Harmonious Fists.
Fish storm.

They're heaving cannons
into Tung Street.
Bubonic tongues poking out
of drains
in Tung Street.

I saw a weeping moon

        floating above

                Kowloon!

Schopenhauer, Oppenheimer.
Gatling guns on Tung Street.
Neon snapped.
The goddess of the sea

on vacation.
Joss sticks on strike.
In the Man Mo Temple
(Hollywood Road)
the god of bureaucracy
at the end of his tether.
The Chew-Chew Massage Parlour
(closed) on Tung Street.

Handmade coffins
tumbling down
Ladder Street.
Possession Street
dispossessed.
Black rain
punishing
Tung Street.

Where's my incense stick?
Where are my ancestors?
Where's the Banyan Tree?
Where's the floating restaurant?
Where's the 7/11 heaven?
I want my Neon back.
Fruitless expiation.
Kneel in front of Tin Hau.

Why am I weeping like a lamb?
Why am I howling like a dog?
Why's my brother on the cross?

Why these dreams of Pelosi?
Where's Clear Water Bay?
Where's my lucky money?
Where's my incense stick?
Burn it! Burn it! Burn it!

Gigi Picetti
Actor, Genoese Activist, Molotov Cocktail

1939–2022

I lived in the caruggi, lived in the Sottoripa
the streets pushing deeper and deeper.

I lived in the vicoli:
lamentation, catastrophe, chicory.

Ubiquitous Gigi would come and go.
He once knew Dario Fo.

I seem to remember Gigi Picetti
had a machete.

The day – in question – was hot and hazy.
He swirled it about

to frighten the piccolo borghese.

Rose of Jericho

I took myself to Saint Sepulchre Cemetery – Jericho.
Several handfuls of the dead.
They fell asleep, outside the walls, in Jericho.

Are you grieving, Margaret, are you grieving?

A curved bench and flowers and an overgrowth.
The Rose of Jericho.
And there lies Benjamin Jowett, Master of Baliol.
He taught Gerard Manley Hopkins.

In the cemetery I was profligate.

I heard the man from Jericho weeping on his archipelago.

I heard the chuckle of the honeysuckle.

Edo-Venezia

for Peter Robinson

Oda Nobunaga
is at the Lido,
admiring the cupolas
from across the water
from the Hotel Excelsior
not yet built.

Gaze upon loveliness.

Metaphysics
and time warps,
fugal
as well as feudal.
Basho on crystal meths.
Turner and Tintoretto
in the mood
for confabulation.
Titian
playing chess
with Hokusai,
the language gap a time hole
and luminosity a religion.
Let my eyes do the talking.

Evanescence.
I shall bring it to you.

The Excelsior's doing well.
The receptionist
(conceived

circa nineteen hundred
and eight)
finds rooms
for Nobunaga
and his entourage.
They were crossing
the Shiranuhi-Kai
(il mare del fuoco misterioso)
and the waves folded –
and the Edo warriors
found themselves

in Venezia / Venice

ヴェネツィア

Nobunaga
can hang his sword
in a sliding wardrobe,
ring Room Service.
They bring
a blood-red aperitivo
with a glazed parasol
poking out

which reminds him
– somehow –
of Sakura
his mistress
that high-spirited girl

with lacquered feet
and sympathetic buttocks
whose mastery of rice balls
has been discussed
on several occasions.

On the long beach
at the Lido
the warriors grip
their Haja-no-Ontachi
(Evil Crushing Blades)
and practise:
swiping at the air
the cupolas
the spires
the white bulls.

Enzo the waiter
looks like a soldier
in Napoleon's army
which will arrive
on the Lido
many years hence,
he carries
a tray of
cappuccinos
to the guests.

Bow low, bow low.
Nobunaga says

We are not monks.
Do not dishonour us.
We are Samurai.
Bring us grappa
if you bring us anything at all.

A gaggle of geese
flies over head.
A homesick warrior
begins
to disembowel himself.
Stop!
There will be time
for disembowelling
    later.

Lunch time on the Lido,
Nobunaga asks for carp.
We can serve clams
or white fish or baccalà.

Hattori Hanzō,
the ghost samurai,
snaps his fingers
and golden carp,
like gladiators
rise to the surface.

The Doge in his gondola.
Madonnas and buddhas

and the bones of St Mark,
and the bones of E.P.
are floating in the Grand Canal.
Prayers in the ghetto.
Shinto in the calle.

Nobunaga says:
We're outflanked.
We'll make our last stand
on the island of Chioggia.
I want Miyamoto and Ito
to check it out.

This is the beginning of history
or the end of history.
The church bells are out of sync.
The ants can't find
a way back to their
nest.

I can smell the puzza
which comes
at the end of the world.
The stink of Venice.

We'll take
the lagoon,
the canals,
the Bridge of Sighs.
Your swords

and armour
are laid out
on the beach.
We have horses,
Kisouma.
Beware
Lord Byron
with his strange
leg,
his singing
bear.

Tree-poles in the water.
Oak in the water.
Briccole:
crucifixes striding
in formation.
Look!
The last Samurai
in battle armour,
ready for battle.
We will fight them
on the beaches.
We'll fight them
in the lagoon.

Camels in St Mark's Square
and ninjas
and tea ceremonies
and romantic trysts

and the Shogun
in Caffè Florian
and Haibun merchants.
The Doge is in his gondola.
Marco Polo gone, gone, gone.

Eduardo Chiossone
writes to Count Enrico di Borbone.

BRICCOLE – LOOK!
The last samurai
waiting for canon ball
and musket.
ACQUA ALTA
and the lagoon police
and the great wave off Kanagawa.

Chianini

I met some bulls on the mountain road.
The godliest bulls I've seen.
And if you saw how wide they opened their eyes!
Please step into our garden of mystery,
our garden of fennel and blood and history.
What beautiful horns you have!
They stopped so I could touch them.

They walked alone, no farm boy, no yapping dog.
Thank you, they said. We know we're beautiful,
oftentimes we see our reflection in the river.
We're Roman you know.
We can remember the centurions and the sweat
and the bathhouse
not that we ever went to the bathhouse
and Jupiter himself.
We're mentioned in the *Georgics* you know.
Virgil ate a wondrous lunch.
It's nice talking to you, I said.
We're quiet bulls, they said, never gregarious
even if Pope Gregory extended his good arm
that day and blessed us.

I suppose – they continue – there's no harm
in chatting on a mountain road, when the sun's out.
Where are you going? I asked.
What a question! they said.
We're going to the slaughterhouse.
If you think we're beautiful that's only the beginning of the story.
I'm not going to the slaughterhouse,

said one of the bulls.
I'm coming to your kitchen.
Do you know where I live?
I guess you have knives and pots and pans and a winding sheet.
I will hide in your freezer like a troubadour.

Wouldn't you prefer to spend more time
wandering over the Umbrian hills,
letting the sun warm your flanks?
We've been wandering for years, wayside traveller.
Singing ballads, chomping grass, on a low heat.
You can't escape your destiny forever.
Dante drooled for a decade because of us.
Didn't he so!
He should have got down to his poem sooner.
Though – to be fair – he made a good job of it.
Didn't he just! said the bull thinking of swinging by.

Umbrian Moon
Ancaiano

At the end of August
the moon fixed itself in the sky
as if a pope were about to die.

It got into the olive trees.
It got into the porcupine.
It got into the stone. Into the guts.

Held its position till morning.
Owl-tremor, dog-bark, cock-crow.
My window my lover.

The blue had gone
and the house was washed in sun.

A cherry tree rattling in the breeze.
A redstart perched on the house.

I saw an eagle soaring upwards,
with a long snake in its mouth.

Divinity

The priest's small
hands roam across
the table. The priest's
small hands
are exceptionally able.
The priest's large head
is full of lore. The
priest's small legs
barely touch the floor.
The priest's wine
cellar is really rather
good. He wants his
guests
to drink the wine they
should. The priest's
plump cook brings
dishes to the table.

The priest's rosary is
an esoteric cable. The
priest's small mouth is
as round
as it is holy. He wants
to be a cardinal.
If only. Only. The
priest's small hands
are clasped
in prayer. He's saying
grace for everybody
there. The priest's
plump cook brings
another round of
dishes. He wants the
guests to satiate their
wishes. Small hands
reaching for escargot,
small creatures
carrying God's cargo.
The small priest likes
Botticelli

and he particularly
likes Handel's
Messiah and the
small priest's not
averse to English
jelly. His typical
recommendation is
transubstantiation.
The priest has read
Diderot and he's read
historical accounts
of Hannibal but the
priest doesn't see
the taking of the
Eucharist as the
action of a cannibal.
The priest's young
mistress pours the
wine. The priest's
small finger touches
the divine.

The Sheer Glory of It

All this – of course – was heaven when I smoked.
Standing under the trees,
my sweet asylum,
resourceful and joyful, and dry.

Once – when I smoked that is –
the people coming up the pavement –
people with great lives ahead,
cheered as I stood there.
A Bohemian, they said. Truly.

Notwithstanding the rain
we observe a man with a cigarette.
Like Baudelaire in the suburbs.
Reeking of nicotine.
Awaiting his horse-pulled limousine.

Speed

One of my students, a rather large girl,
came along for a tutorial.
You should be reading this! she said
slamming down a copy
of Rupi Kaur's latest book.

When the rather large girl had gone
I chucked the book across the room
and for a moment I was struck
by the way it travelled in slow motion –

as the bin got nearer, however, and nearer,
it speeded up.

Fruit Bat Villas

I thought there was a cricket wicket.
The grass was rolled and cut.

A net – or two – for practice.

The players
dressed in black,
cloaked.
A contest – crepuscular.
Ashes.
Dust.

Back in the day
teams travelling down under
spent weeks at sea.

Dinners.
Dress codes.
Tinned fruit.
The dark night of the soul.
Sleep.

A little batting on the deck.

Pace bowlers hanging by their feet.
All-rounders.
Umpires whistling in the dark.
Leg spinners upside down.
Full of guile, malodorous.

Tobleronia

Looking out of the window
looking at the snow
made you feel drowsy.
The train trundled along.
You dozed off.
You were asleep too long.

You missed that little village
on the hill
with its glühwein and chocolate fruit.
You missed the Toblerone factory
and the ornate clock.
You missed the Kunst Halle
and the Rathouse.

The train crossed the Rhine,
crossed back again.
You missed that flick of sunshine.

You missed Dorf Kitsch
the polyglottal border town
where everyone is rich.

You missed the pike fillets
battered in beer
and the chocolate cake
covered in cream
and the local yodelling team

You're awake now.
You're at the end of the line.
The snow's thickened.
There's a storm on the way.

There are no trains back for a while.
You'd not wanted to travel
this far north.
You put your face to the window.
Welcome to Wankdorf.

Tree in the Rain

Go in peace,
go with joy into the soft rain
which never ends.
Rain without end.
Go in peace
under the rain:
the Liffey Arms, O'Rourke's,
the horses.
Sundays without end.
Rain without end.

Some of us make our way
to the memory tree.
Desmond has a list of the dead
and he says a few words
about each one
though even as he speaks
the list is growing.
This could go on for a long time
he says
and the rain is forever creeping
down my neck.

Dermot plays the flute
and the priest
who looks as if he could do
with a Sunday roast
is asked to say a few words:
Let the souls of the departed
make their way to the heavenly

father without hold up
or hindrance
or unnecessary delay.
Amen to that we say.
And Killian reads a poem.
Some of us are holding umbrellas.
Finn says there's a rumour
the rain might scoot away
tomorrow,
or the day after that.
For a moment,
praise the lord,
I see a light
hovering above Finn's head.

The Judas Tree

I want to be the glitter
in the glittering sea

the last shepherd
under the Judas Tree.

I want to be the Tiger Balm
on the prophet's head.

I want to be Oscar Wilde
in that enormous bed.

I want to be the casket
in the cathedral crypt.

The hermeneutic hermit
with that arcane script.

I want to be the martyr
stripped and whipped.

I want to be the glitter
in the glittering sea

the last shepherd
under the Judas Tree.

My Teeth Are Flayed

They drop bombs. I lose teeth.
My mouth's become the Gaza Strip.
My people humble people.
My teeth humble teeth.
My mouth a dead mouth
of carious teeth that
cannot spit, that has no bread to eat.
My mouth is full of body parts.
I eat concrete, cities, nothing.
Black milk of daybreak we gulp at night.
We drink and we drink.
Dead people humble people.
Goodbye Palestine.
My teeth are flayed.
Anesthetise my mouth.
Anesthetise my house.
Gaza rhymes with Gethsemane.
Gaza rhymes with Gehenna.
My teeth are violinists
with snapped off fingers.
My teeth are flayed like Jesus.

Old Leg

There's a stump at the end of the wall
where the gleeful dogs all piss.

I watch them through the window.
Their owners sheepish.

It's not me cocking the old leg, the old leg.
I wave like Charles de Gaulle.

Who can resist the pissing wall?

from Please Don't Bomb the
Ghost of my Brother (2023)

Love in the Time of Corona

Lockdown, the sails hunger for a wind.
Violins in the rafters. In the middle flat Ella Fitzgerald sings
Clams do it, oysters do it, jellyfish do it.

The love microbe slips off its bathrobe.

Be not afeard. The house is full of noises.
Sounds that wake you in the night.
Beds and sofas pull up anchor. Headboards
bang on walls. Sheets hang from windows,
salty sails for a tailwind.
Lazarus foreshadowed the resurrection.
The blonde goes down on the boy's erection.

The crow's nest sways.
The Bulgarians set up post-communist love regimes.
Such energy.
The house judders and swoons and moans.

I look at the moon
because the moon loves being looked at.

On dry land there is no touch. Touchless.
Daily bulletins of the dead.

In this house molluscs and cracked ceilings.
Neighbours crack each other open.
I watch a film about O. J. Simpson's glove.

We've become Wilhelm Reich's Orgone Energy Accumulator,
Model 2.
The gasket blows in the engine room.

Notes are slipped under my door.
One says Don't be the asshole on the Good Ship Lollipop.

One says I love you baby.

One night my door is knocked upon.
I open it an inch and see the platinum girl.
Her lips have kissed so much
they're puffed up like a boxer's.

We have no sugar in the crow's nest captain.
I fill her cup with sugar. I give her sugar:

slave sugar   love sugar   sugar-sugar.

Zoom Time

One of the most wretched things about lockdown
was being zoomed into hundreds of well-lit
middle class homes whose impeccable taste
made me feel down at heel, even shitty,
as if I were Edward Lear sitting at the table of Lord Stanley
trying to make the soup not trickle into my beard
and called upon at any moment to entertain (a singular
fellow.)

There was an Old Person of Cromer who stood on one leg
reading Homer . . .

2

Artfully arranged bookshelves frame the background
of every Zoomer, the libraries of the baby boomer –
Sometimes I catch the titles on the spines: Proudhon
The 120 Days of Sodom, Plato's critique of humour.

3

The undoubted advantage of a Zoom conference,
as far as I can tell, is that no one
has banned smoking although I have to admit
that when I took out a cigarette which I did
without thinking, I am after all sitting in my room,

not book-lined but nevertheless containing
an impressive collection of revolving ashtrays,
so as to lift the familiar stick to my wanting lips,
I understood I was smoking in the face
of a global plague and suddenly I was afraid.

4

The don from Cambridge is explaining that the poem
he is about to read, I fear it won't be short,
required the reading of one thousand five hundred books.
I suspect that behind him in that donnish room
we can see the one thousand five hundred books.

5

Oh fellow Zoomers
how much lovelier to think of a theatre
playing THE SHOW CAN'T GO ON!

An empty stage with blood-red seats
and balconies with strips of gold.
A man walks across the stage
and stops and turns and smiles –
Very old school, *ja*, he says.

You think life disappointing?
We have no troubles here! Here life is beautiful.

The girls are beautiful. the orchestra is beautiful.
And for a tantalising moment we can see the girls
and we can hear the orchestra
like the shadow of a coachman outside a hermitage.

Death – please – thou shalt die.

6

There's a young couple in one of the boxes
sitting entwined in comfortable repose.
The man's hand is on the woman's knee
and I'm wondering what would happen
if, in the comfort of their sitting room,
they forget that in panoptic mode
fifty pairs of eyes can see how
knee touching leads to greater acts
of intimacy; their caresses more ardent,
more urgent – O Corinna, Corona!
Someone has turned up the wattage,
some unexpected zoomer frottage . . .

7

I notice the professor from St Petersburg
has left his chair and I lean forward to see
if I can make out titles in that august language.
He has several shelves of Gogol
(for a fleeting moment I thought he had the tales

of Nikolai Vasilyevich Google)
which brings me a sudden unbridled joy.
I too will leave my place, if only to return,
like Banquo at the feast of Zoom –
and let the viewers admire my wall of nothing,

> *I saw the shadow of a coachman*
> *who with the shadow of a brush*
> *did clean the shadow of a coach*

Radio Requests

I lost last year my wife of fifty years, sweet Mavis.
Would you, could you play some Miles Davis?

My partner's gotten Alzheimer's.
The days have shrunk.
Spread some joy with Thelonious Monk.

I lost my father, the days are darker.
Could you play some Charlie Parker?

I kicked my addiction to cocaine.
If you could play anything by John Coltrane
I'd open another bottle of champagne.

A kumquat for a quintet.
                              A jazz band in a dream land!

I switched gender. I call myself Cherry.
I'd dance across the room if you played Chuck Berry.

Last year was a train wreck.
Time, surely, for Dave Brubeck.

The days are grey, the sky is gloopy.
Energise us with Fela Kuti.

Last year my husband was so unkind
I ran away.
Could you play something by Billie Holiday?

I popped the question to my girlfriend Jean.
A thumbs up!
We're gagging for some Bunky Green.

My auntie's knitting Kashmiri shawls.
A sudden blast of Biggie Smalls?

After thirty years of marriage
my wife threw in the towel –
(leaping off a bridge) –
Oh Maisy! Maisy! Maisy!
She was always partial to Count Basie.

Shall we, shan't we, should we, let's.
Give us something by Stan Getz.

This year I gave birth to Jerome.
Almost anything please by Nina Simone!

It was our first wedding anniversary last year
(I don't normally tell people this,
I met my husband at Walmart . . .)
We lowered the blinds,
a tip-top afternoon with Django Reinhart.
Would you? Could you? Should you?

I grabbed it online and paid the acquisition fee!
Bring on the trumpets, Dizzy Gillespie.

I recently qualified as a Level Two Undertaker.
Please play My Funny Valentine by Chet Baker.

We lost dear Max on Boxing Day.
Our loving selfless Dachshund dog.
Could we hear the voice of Karin Krog?

My dentist went completely mad
and pulled out all my teeth.
I now make a weird sucking noise
which goes quite well with 'Tootie' Heath.

Last year I had a stroke.
I would like to listen to some Elmo Hope.

Last year another breakdown, I was sent away . . .
Reel me back with Sidney Bechet.

A kumquat for a quintet.
                                    A jazz band in a dream land!

Last month I gave up and laid down
for the last time my weary head.
Could you play The Grateful Dead?

Duck Corner

I'll meet you at Duck Corner.

                                 I'll be riding Gauloises
my newly acquired horse.

He used to clop along
Boulevard Saint-Michel
singing *Le Monde Entier Fait Boum!*

with Simone de Beauvoir
and Jean-Paul Sartre.

Of course –

Now it's Duck Corner . . .

In fact the only person who isn't there
is you!

I like it when you're late.
Even better when you're dead –

So déjà vu.
I should be stricken by remorse.

If my mouth could open wider
I'd smoke the entire horse.

Have you noticed
our meetings at Duck Corner never work out?

The hooves of the horse are hoofing.
It's so wretchedly déjà vu.

Have you read *The Magnificent Smoking Horse*
by Albert Camus?

Better Now or Better Now or Better Never?

Can you put your chin on the rest please. Super.
Look straight ahead into the light, if you can see the light.
Can you see the light? I didn't think you could.
If it makes you feel better 90 percent of my patients
can see the light. You'll have to imagine the light.
Can you look to the left? To the right. Look up, look down.
And now straight ahead. Super. You can sit back now.
Would you like a mint?

I'm going to put some drops in your eyes.
Might sting a bit. Look up. Super. Again. Super.
Can you read any of the letters on the chart?
I didn't think so. If it makes you feel better
90 percent of my patients can read the first two rows.
Can you put your chin back on the rest. Super.
Look straight ahead into the light you cannot see
and when the orange mist lifts you'll notice a road
which appears to be leading to eternity.

Can you see the long road which appears
to be leading to eternity? Yes I can actually. I can.
Beautiful. Does it remind you of that song
by Talking Heads, We're on the road to nowhere?
Super. Keep looking down that long road.
Is it clearer now, or now? Is it clearer now, or now?
Or the same? The same. No – clearer now.
I can see a balloon. You can see a balloon?

Beautiful. Look closely at the balloon and tell me
whether you can see a person in a wicker basket.

You might like to think of the 1870 siege of Paris,
the Prussians are at the gates, elephant soup
is on the menu, the French are climbing into balloons,
trying to flee. Can you see anyone in the wicker basket?

I can see someone in the wicker basket. Can you tell me
who that person is? It's rather blurred. Of course.
If it makes you feel better 80 percent of my patients
only see a balloon and have never heard of
the Franco-Prussian War and would not be having
this conversation. Wicker basket my arse . . .

Better now, or now, or now, or never?
Try again, better now, or now? Better now.
Beautiful. Are you able to tell me who the person
in the wicker basket is? Strange as it may sound
I think it's Priti Patel. Well, well, well
it is Priti Patel! You can sit back now.

There's a knock at the door.
The ophthalmologist's assistant comes in with a note.
She gives it to him and slips out. Did you notice anything
unusual about my assistant? She was somewhat blurred.
Of course she was. He calls out a name and
the assistant comes back. Is she clearer now, or now?
Clearer now? Or the same? Clearer now. Super –

Let me ask you again, did you notice anything unusual?
Yes, she looks like Priti Patel! Doesn't she just!
Would you like another mint?

[46]

I've examined your retinal scans.
I'm sorry to say you have an eye disease
called Priti-Patelitis. It's quite serious.
We need to check out its rate of progress.
If we diagnose early we might be able to slow it down.
You're still likely to have unpleasant side effects.
Have to live with it I'm afraid.

Can you put your chin back on the rest. Super.
And could you hold this hand pump
in your right hand. Super-duper.
We're going to watch an optic video simulator
called Corneal Protection Level Three.

Look at the long road which appears to be
going absolutely nowhere and when you hear the beep
you'll find your plane of vision inundated
with microscopic Patels, some striding out
of White Hall looking smug, some marching
through Jerusalem with members of the Likud,
some leaping up and down like Rumple what's his name.

As the eye pressure increases
a miniature Patel will seek to penetrate
your nasolacrimal duct
and push into the hippocampus.

Try and zap Home Secretary Patel
the bat out of hell
by squeezing the hand pump.

Are you ready?

Beautiful. You can sit back now.
Shot of brandy?
Might as well enjoy things whilst you can.

He calls for his assistant.
Could you run these off please. Beautiful.
We'll have the results in twenty minutes.
Do you mind if we listen to some Ravel?

The Crossing

The lone stag's crossing a field.
He's done with rutting.
Outside Snape Maltings
he listens to Alexander Gadjiev.
He's got Chopin in his head.
He misses the girls.
He's missing an antler.
The sky is blood-red.
The sonata was perfect.

He's always had a thing
about New York.
He slips into the water
at Bawdsey.
His wounds are cauterised.
He's swimming
to Old Felixstowe.

He curls up in the bowels
of the ship
like Rimbaud.
He's not sure how things will go.
The stowaway stag.
He's going to start again.
He'd like some music.
He'd like to play the cello.
He'd really like a cigar.

Escalator City

Last month you'd never heard of it –
Now you're there hook, line and sinker
stepping onto an escalator
which is going up and up and up
the sunlight streaking your face –

and sometimes – what longing – you glimpse a city
(a real city) Berlin, Athens, London, Budapest, Rome.

Weren't you glad when you reached
the gates of Hyderabad?

Now you're rising
and then, as if it were a game
of snakes and ladders,
you're going down . . .

A moment of reflection – oh no, not that – *reflection!*

One moment you're up like a Tiramisu.
The next you're going down like a plum pudding.

By the way
it's not the sort of place you can get away from in a hurry.

There was, I think, an entrance –

Welcome.

We Appreciate Slow-Walkers, Non-Talkers
and – please note – Staring Is Forbidden!

No point running up the escalator
because you imagined you saw something
plucked from the world – a white horse say,
a house with a garden and some befuddled shed.
Saying shed makes you feel giddy.

Shed, shed – giddy – giddy – oh!

Some people are sent to Escalator City
as a punishment – *I did something wrong.*

No one used to lie in bed saying:
Please don't send me to Escalator City.
I'd rather shove a stick in my eye.

You've been sentenced to a month in Escalator City.
Oh weep for me.
You've been sentenced to six months.
Oh weep for me even more.
Up and up, in search of redemption.
The city on the hill with moving walkways –

Tiramisu with whips!

Some come to Escalator City for therapy.
The rhythms of ascent (Apotheosis)

and descent (Gehenna) etc etc will nudge
the frontal cortex into the right position
and have an improving effect
on the buttocks – a cosmic re-alignment.
Two months of therapeutic escalators
and you will step into the horizontal world
like an evangelical toaster.

You will be new – like a wedding gift.

A *walking miracle*.

Sometimes the warmest aromatic winds
greet you on the escalator
and your private parts buzz with satisfaction.
On those occasions the escalators
are full of tantalising opportunities.
The next escalator sends an Artic wind
which stops you in your tracks.
Oh Lord Shiva what have I done?
Have I not suffered enough?
I'm afraid not, there's always more to come.
The steps of the escalator
are onto you like the teeth of a shark.

There are more announcements:
Escalators are moving pieces of machinery.
Please hold onto the handrail.
Please do not stare – don't fall asleep.
No kissing, no horse play – no horses.

No inappropriate touching.
Please be aware you are about to step off
the escalator – there will be a jolt
as if you were about to leap off a turret.
No turret to leap off – concentrate.
See it, say it, shag it (shag what?)
Escalator City would seem a shagless kind of place.
Sometimes a pigeon zips through.
Sometimes music.
The least interesting songs of Steely Dan.
Some days everybody looks like Bamber Gascoigne.
Sometimes an advert – Are you feeling tired?

Yes!

There are walkways between the escalators
and designated food stations
where they serve durian fruit
and beef cheek with pearl barley (Paul Bailey?)
and reconstituted cattle burgers,
whose gherkins were consecrated by the pope.

And there are lavatorial breaks which are,
without doubt, the most agreeable thing.
Your buttocks are washed with kumquat spray
and dried to perfection by a Kyoto breeze.
You look forward to your next evacuation.
(Montaigne was fond of his bowels.)
The excrement is sucked into the oubliette
which goes down and down and down

to a state-of-the-art recycling plant
and which then climbs up and up and up
in a Nietzschean loop of everlastingness.

Not a City but a Beautiful Catastrophe

Nice sitting in Bar Barracuda in the Sottoripa
under the porticos, watching the city
come to life: the fish stalls, the hum
of the sopraelevata, the early-rising priests,
the cupola of Santa Maria delle Vigne
floating in vapour, the addicts, the hustlers,
the pimps, the street sellers, the matelots,
the fish-fryers, an endless unveiling
of gestures, and the Irishman
standing on his tower in Caricamento.
By eight o'clock the sun's broken through.
It's going to be a long, long day.

Piazza Della Lepre

There's a black door
in Piazza Della Lepre
with neoclassical figures.
The stairs lead up to a knocking shop,
at the very top.
The best in the city, oh what ceilings!
There's no lift.
You must walk up the slate stairs.
The stairs are steep.
Not everyone can:
heart seizure, ennui, brain softening
and some who do
never put their nose in the piazza again,
extinguished – it would seem – by rapture.
Number 9, Piazza Della Lepre.
Books have been written
and songs have been sung.
Any man of that age
would have taken their pleasure there
back in the day.
They were young.
They didn't walk up the stairs.
They – more or less – ran.

Mistress
Sestri Levante

I arranged to meet Gloria at the Gran Caffè Tritone.
I knew she'd be late so I drank a coffee and waited.
She was sitting there! I hadn't recognised her!
She'd put on a lot of weight. She was suffering.
As if some old unloved aunt had dropped by.
We kissed – once, twice – and made our way to the sea.
There was a man from Dakar on the beach
selling shells to put around the neck
as well as bangles and beads and silver bracelets
for the ankles and he thought I was Gloria's
husband – *marito* – and he asked me whether
I'd like some henna on my lady's body
and Gloria looked like a holy cow
covered with baubles and trinkets which swayed
and gleamed in the sun.
The man asked, Do you have children?
No, she said and he touched his heart (I'm sorry)
saying it was God's will and he told us
about the woman in Bangladesh whose womb
had been turned into a durian fruit.
You had to hold your nose as you drew near, he said
but the fruit of her womb was ecstasy.
(Some of this, I think, was lost in translation.)
We walked into the sea – the man with shells shouting
Great Fortune! Great Fortune! and you might have thought
Gloria was a boat as she pushed into the waves
with shells around her neck and bracelets around her
ankles and the henna smudged a little by the water,
and her feet were fused together and she shucked off
the cancer and the fibromyalgia and the weight,

and the girl who used to work at Principe Station
making platform change announcements
who for eighteen years was Lanfranco's mistress
became what the Italians call a sirena.
She looked at the shore, turning seawards,
swimming out of the Bay of Fables,
the white church tolling its bells across the town
and the coco bello man shouting *Coco bello!*
Coco bello! And that same morning a boy
from the village was killed on his motorbike.

Quartet in C

The Cicada Armada fetched up in June:
a relentless hypnotic barrage.

Tutus

I came home to the Cicada Youth Orchestra
and I lay on the floor.
Our old mutt Bobby lay down beside me
panting.
When evening came
the fireflies, having put on their tutus, cavorted.

The CIA

Sectioned, I was sent to the Cicada Lunatic Asylum.
Doctor Coppola signed the papers.
His patients, he explained,
were beleaguered by obsessions.
Hence the cicadas which colonised the trees
in the great courtyard.
We were encouraged to adore them.
This was Doctor Coppola's radical way
of defying insanity, he was known across Europe.
It wasn't easy at first.
Sbagliando si impara.
Practice makes perfect.
Imagine locked wards of relatively decent people
flapping their tongues.
Even the cicadas thought we were cicadas.
Saturdays
Doctor Coppola conducted his monomaniacal troupe
from the gazebo.
People came from Spoleto: wooden benches,
jugs of wine, hand-rolled cigarettes.

Bravissimo! Bravissimo!

Pimpinella

After ten years in the Cicada Lunatic Asylum
I was cured. Doctor Coppola signed the papers
and was almost brotherly. After a decade of cicadas
you may call me by my Christian name.
We are releasing you into Umbria – the lungs of Italy –
and he shook me by the hand. *Tante cose!*
I walked into the world with a healed mind
and when I felt hunger
Lanfranco the shepherd fed me on yesterday's bread.
His sheep had left him but he chanced upon them,
alive – yes – but they had suffered a change.
And peasant women who conversed with mushrooms
and an English-speaking woman called Daria
who'd long ago eaten fish with Doctor Jagger.
And a German who showed me his lederhosen.
I walked past medieval turrets, I saw castles
on the tops of mountains and heard tales
of the Knights Templar. I was never alone:
wild boar, red fox, deer, goats, bears shuffling down
from the Apennines and I delighted in the dragonfly
and the gecko and lovelorn donkeys
and mystical mules. Stray dogs befriended me
and I swam naked in the rivers, patrolled by kingfishers.
And lay under the lavendered blanket of the night
listening to wolves.
Somewhere swallows swooping over Trasimeno.
I faced the sun, the winds, the snow.
Strangers would give me a shed, a bed,
a plate of strangozzi, a suckling pig
and I came across villages wrecked by earthquakes

high on pimpinella, lentil flowers,
mustard flowers, poppies, legousia and fennel
and by the stream the lord prince, the Purple Heron.
I spent a week with a hermit. A month. A year.
Then I reached Bastardo
where I felt at home. They found me a house,
one up, one down, and because I spoke cicada fluently
I asked for a gentle symphony.
A black cat rubbed against my leg.
I had my own place – the Small House in Bastardo –
and I wrote to Doctor Coppola as he'd instructed,
without using his first name, I couldn't somehow,
even though I tried. Doctor Coppola, Doctor Coppola.
As promised he sent me a mental health worker
who was an olive-grower.
Eat these, he said, the olives of redemption
as if a green god were caressing my spleen
with the wing of a butterfly.

Please Don't Bomb the Ghost of My Brother

He's riding a white horse.
I was going to say he was riding into the forest.
It's more like a wood, a large wood
with sycamore trees and silver birch
and if you look you can see a Weeping Willow.
There are deer in the undergrowth
watching carefully
and there are a lot of small animals.
He's talking to the horse and patting its neck.
There's no one else around
and the wood has a beguiling music.

The horse breaks into a canter.
Rabbits listen and twitch.
An oyster catcher flies overhead.
And coming into view a long-winged buzzard.

The horse slows and steps into the river –
He's a good horse, my brother's a good horseman.
Now they're getting out on the other side
where there are fewer trees.
The ghost of my brother finds a glade.
There must be a score of white horses.
There's sun light and there's a breeze.
The horses drink from the water.
And the ghosts, soldiers like my brother,
strip off and throw themselves into the lake.
Some lie on their backs.

My brother has slipped from view.
I bet you he's taken a big breath
kicked his legs and plunged down deep.
The horses stand under a tree.
My brother's horse is whinnying.

Thud

The blind boy had a lover
who was ravenous. A raven?
How would he know?
Her mouth hungry as a puppy
her arms so plucky, lucky.

He couldn't see whether
he was on the Inner Circle or the Outer.

He couldn't see the People's Palace.
He couldn't see Buchanan Street.
He couldn't see the Clyde.

He could hear the wind. He could hear the gulls.
He could hear the thud of a ball.
He could hear the chanting –
his lover tied herself to his foot
her hair was black of course.

NOX PERPETUA!

He wanted to make a film. He enrolled on a course.
Federico Fellini, Rosselini, Bolognini, Pasolini
and Stevie Wonder rolled into one.

The *mise-en-abyme*, the universal scream.
He was interrogating the existential hole
not some cameo role –

He hatched a plan and flipped a fugue –

Break into the Kelvingrove Gallery
under the cover of night, perpetual night
and slip away with Dalí's Crucifixion.

No thorns, no blood, no nails
suspended above a lake –
ready to slide into the lake.

First they went to Mother India to eat –
to work out the ins and outs.
Kenny slapped a paratha
round his face, an instant balaclava.

Powder your face with sunshine
Put on a great big smile . . .

They lowered Christ of Saint John of the Cross
onto the boy's back.
He had broad shoulders,
his calf muscles strengthened
by amorous trysts.

Tricky getting out of the door.

And he walked down Argyle Street
as if it were Palm Sunday
with sixty million pounds of Salvador Dalí
        on his back –

Tricky getting back into the flat

with Christ of Saint John of the Cross on his back –
The neighbours gawping.

But there's always a chance
with Christ on your back
of a MIRACOLO fast track.
The boy got his sight back!

Raven lay on her back, aflutter. Ecstatic boy.
He was the lead man in his own film.
He'd acquired the gift of sight.
He'd thumbed his nose at the police.
He'd escaped with the Crucifixion.
There was trouble, however, with his erection.

He clambered onto the raven
like a winged aardvark
heavy, locked in, soft –

No nails in his hands
Christ slid down the cross
into the lovers' bed.
A ménage a trois. A thud.

A kitsch triptych.

Imagine there's no heaven.
Quite easy if you try.

A short film –

it won several prizes.

L'Osservatore Romano
said it was shot through
with a slither of evil.

Madonna dell' Orto

for Wendy

The vaporetto lurched and groaned.
The water rising, splashing the tables
of the café laid out on the front.
The Madonna dell' Orto.
The boatman lines up his boat.
People holding tight as they got off,
as they got on.
A cream motoscafo thumping past.
The lagoon that day was a garden under grey.
Rain coming.
The currents firing fish,
seabirds overhead,
the fruits of the sea,
the dead rising to the surface.
We saw Stravinsky and Brodsky,
we saw Diaghilev and Pound.
The water had given them their shape
their musculature, their purpose.
Half fish, half men.
Some had re-acquired their beards.
The lagoon reeled with the violins
of Olga Rudge.
Pound's jaws wide as a barracuda's:
snapping at the bream
snapping at the poles in the water
snapping at his reputation.

The Magnificence of Death

We could hear the hooves of the Mongols –
our walled city was hanging fruit, hanging low.
I could see my head on a pole –
Our bowmen had slipped away in the night.

We could kneel down and beg mercy and then
have our heads cut off or we could have our heads
cut off without the bother of kneeling down.

What say you?

There was some opium left. I think I'll have that.
The beetroot merchant had fled too.
The smartest thing he'd ever done –

Although we have no cannon ball, the captain said
we have beets the size of giants' gonads.
Let's boil them and make a pool of blood.

And when the Mongols climb the ramparts
we'll let the beetroot rain upon them.

Is that some kind of joke captain?

The reason I'm standing here
and you're standing there
is because I passed the Imperial Exams.
I read Li Po's treatise on warfare
at least most of it –
Do you have a better idea?

I rather liked peeling the beets
even as the hooves got nearer
occasionally having a bite,
not bad, not great either.

Before long we could see the Mongol flags.
Water ran down our soldiers' legs
even as we cracked jokes to keep our spirits up.
Have you heard the one about the Mongol
and the Archbishop of Budapest?

My hands were bloodied like a murderer's.
No one could say we lived dull lives.

And the musicians reached for instruments
and played a piece long before its time
that would be copied by some doleful goth
a name like Beet-Hosan many years hence
called Speaking Unto Nations.
If we could only speak to the Mongols
and ask them to go away.

I don't know how or why I know this
or what prompted the court musicians to refrain
from their usual din but thank God they did.
A moment of genius, a moment of terror.

By now the Mongols were catapulting
the severed heads of concubines –

I was in a reverie:
as fragrant as the Emperor's Vale of Stars.

Wet-cheeked I remembered afternoons
of gentle spooning followed by
the choicest parts of armadillo.
Sweet faraway non-Mongolian days!

Oi soldier, concentrate –
Pierced by arrows
my head not mounted on a pole
(getting there . . .)
we let them have it.

The Committal

IM: Steadman Stephen Thompson (1966–2022), Writer

They dug a deep hole and the brothers filled it
with the help of a dumper truck
which dropped the earth next to the grave.
It was hot and the brothers wiped themselves
with towels and took a little rum
to give themselves heft, and a great aunt
– veiled – read aloud from her psalm book even though
Jimmy Cliff's Many Rivers to Cross was playing on a stereo.
Her voice was pure, and once into her stride she sang
Amazing Grace, how sweet the sound that saved a wretch like me.
And the brothers smoked weed to stay in the spirit groove.
It took more than an hour to fill the hole.
It was an act of love, it was an act of suffering.
The black mourners were dressed in black:
top hats, Rasta caps, suits, some as sharp as
the Tonton Macoutes: soldiers of the rugged cross,
soldiers of a higher power.

It has pleased Almighty God to take him from this world.
We therefore commit his body to the ground,
earth to earth, ashes to ashes, dust to dust.
I am the resurrection and the life to come.
The words rolled off the vicar's tongue.

Kass – Stephen's white 'missus' – at the graveside
taken in by the Jamaican Brotherhood, the Jamaican Sisterhood.
Her grief encircled.
As the flowers were placed on the grave
'To know him was to love him'
I saw Stephen slipping through the gravestones

towards the wood. He was moving fast
clutching *Love in the Time of Cholera*.

He wasn't going to lie down in the London Cemetery.
Some of him would lie down, some would get the hell out:
relax a while, a flight to Athens, the boat to Ithaca.

He's slipping into mythical water, washing off the dust.
They're grilling fish on the beach.

Oh Stephen, great writer, dear friend:
finish that book on Marcus Garvey.
There's always a beginning, there's never an end

from Heat Wave (2020)

Lesson Plan

Walk with purpose into the room.
Bamboozle, baffle, kick-box.

Hand out Bulgarian poems.
Cite Spinoza. Invoke Foucault.

Retreat. Change city. Sleep a little.

Whoopsee

It was late Sunday evening
and I was on the Northern Line
and if the train was not exactly empty
there was enough floor space
for anyone who had a desire to move
their left leg out, their left leg in.

I seem to remember
Leonard Cohen's 'Dance with Me
to the End of Love' sobbed and

bobbed in my head.

I had a small suitcase on wheels
full of exam papers
which I had spent a week marking
with a strange intensity
as if I had taken that drug
which makes you concentrate
very hard and for hours at a stretch.

A small suitcase on wheels
full of exam papers
all marked and ready to go.

I was holding my suitcase
in the way you hold a dog,
quite gently, by its collar –
(there's a good dog, there's a good suitcase . . .)
but I must have taken my hand away.

It was then that the woman opposite me
shouted *Whoopsee!*

Who nowadays. I thought, goes
around shouting *Whoopsee?*

A middle-aged woman, a little crimped,
glasses and a milk-white coat,
a rather casual coat if you will.

Whoopsee!

And I turned to see the suitcase
on wheels moving at quite a pace
along the carriage of the train.

At first I started chasing it.
I had spent an entire week
working on those papers
but the train was
at quite a tilt

and the suitcase was
stretching its legs
imagining a moment
that the suitcase had legs.
I guess the wheels were its legs.

The suitcase was moving at such a pace
I just stood and watched it

as it passed into the next carriage
and continued its way not without grace
down the length of the train.

Occasionally I could hear
from afar, therefore slightly
muffled, some other weirdo
shouting *Whoopsee* . . .

It chose a clean path
through the middle of the train
shooting along as if
it had decided that instead
of being called a suitcase on wheels
it would call itself Thanatos.

The suitcase on wheels
(or Thanatos-on-wheels if you prefer)
full of exam papers hurtling
towards the end of the train.

It was as if my life-long myopia had lifted.
I could see everything with
such clarity, how beautiful it was to see!

How small that case
how redolent with sheen.

All that concentration. All that invigilation.

The end of the train opened
and the suitcase on wheels, *little Thanatos!*
dropped into the flames
as if it were a luminous detail
from that garden of earthly delights.

The University of Lanyard

Reasonable people are wearing lanyards. White collar ponies. *Clop! Clop!*
How are you? I'm good. At what though? Actually, I'm rather good
at wearing a lanyard. I wear it on the way home, in the train. It's so,
well you know, corporate and lanyard-y. Don't you have one?
I did, I took it off and threw it away. Actually I popped it on
the neck of a goat. Or some long-haired prophet. Or maybe I stuck it up
the Dean's arse. Anyway I stack shelves now, or make lattes.
I have a tattoo on my inner thigh which says A SEASON IN HELL.
Even hell needs a lanyard. Hell is a lanyard. Love is a lanyard. God
is a lanyard. God is great. God is a neck-jiving, hip-swinging lanyard.

Shirley High Street

The Mutant Mile

I always thought the end of Shirley High Street
was the drop at the world's end. I know the maps
say differently but what are maps if not lies?
I tend to believe what I see with my eyes.
Shirley High Street is not without its horror –
I've seen Otto Dix weeping in Chicken City.
I've seen Otto Dix limping to the Chemist's.
He needed cod liver oil. He needed a bottle of *Cauchemar*.

If you walked to the end of the High Street you'd fall
off the world, that's what I thought, what's wrong with that?

It's a slow, exacting, Via Crucis.
A wailing wall, so many crazies in an urban wilderness.
Turkish barbers, Cash Converters, pawnbrokers.
Care in the community. Which means nothing.
I've seen a man with a bird cage on his head.
He had grown a beak. His eau de cologne
was Eau de Bird Shit, Eau de Mutant . . .
I've seen a gypsy leading a white mare.
It was the loveliest thing.
If you can travel to the heart of darkness
you can travel to the end of Shirley High Street.

I've seen Otto Dix harangued by a kebab.
I've seen Otto Dix wearing a gas mask.
For years I walked three quarters down, listened
to the ships' calls, listened to a wind

which wasn't a wind, a windless wind if you will.
It's not like Niagara Falls, no spray, nothing.
And then more nothing followed by nothing
followed by some Ravel, which is a boon.

Today I walked to the end of the road
and there was a shop selling parachutes.
I didn't buy one, I just carried on.
There was no drop. More of the same.
They changed the name. Shirley High Street
became Coleridge Crescent. I wish there had been a drop.

I Know When To Stay In

Is that Mr Standard? the girl asks.
It's easier nowadays to say yes.
What sort of day are you having?
An average sort of day, I guess.
Oh that's nice, she says, I like average days.
Yes, I say, average is the new fantastico.
Average is the new Saturday night. Are you ready?
Mr. Standard! She laughs awkwardly.

I start quoting Davie Bowie
because he's quotable and because
he's dead. Davie Bowie is dead. Can that be true?
And who can bear to be forgotten? I say.
Mr Standard we won't forget you.
That's why we've rung you, we like ringing you.
Yes, I've noticed.

And then I say
Do you like pieces of machinery, mine shafts?
things like that? I've not given much thought
to mine shafts, I don't usually deal with them,
she says. Would you like to speak to my manager?
I don't want to speak to anybody.
Then I say, almost happy now,
I know when to go out, I know when to stay in,
get things done.

Mr Standard you're exactly
the kind of person we like, she says,
a throb in her voice. Thank you. And you know what?

What? she says. I feel tragic like I'm Marlon Brando.
Mr Standard, you really should speak to my manager,
his name's Keith. Scary monsters super Keith.
And then I say, my voice quite different now:
Oh my little China girl! Oh Mr. Standard! she replies.

Hey, you shouldn't mess me with me, I say,
I'll ruin everything you are. I'll give you television.
Television! Mr Standard, we're calling about
PPI – your Payment Protection Insurance.
Now listen here, I say, I stumble into town
like a sacred cow, visions of Swastikas in my head.

Sixty People with Flickering Lamps

Bury me at night
bury me in some English churchyard.

Let there be some crooning
Bessie Smith will do.

Let there be some Frederick Delius.

Let there be flasks of alcohol
let there be a clear-eyed manic bat,

and let there be a priest
hauled out of retirement.

Let there be something macaronic
a good old crack of the Teutonic.

Let there be Baron Osterhagen
with a gin and tonic.

Let there be a wooden cricket ball
let me swing low, sweet chariot.

Turkey Blues

There were nice admin ladies in the Liberal Arts Building.
They wanted to know if I'd seen the campus turkeys.
Do they sing to you in the morning? Awake Visiting Professor!
There's no need for an alarm clock when you have
a phalanx of swaggering turkeys fornicating on the college lawns.
Time to wash and dress – high fives for getting dressed – and
time for an American breakfast: a plate of waffles? scrambled
eggs? and coffee which doesn't taste like coffee yet so much of it.
Then walk in a professorial manner to the tower
which is like a beige smack across the face. It's almost bracing.

I had noticed there were no windows on the turkey side
but had imagined, if I'd imagined anything, that the light
of Montana would push through elsewhere like a victory
snatched out of the jaws of defeat, like the cavalry turning up
to rescue Custer at the battle of Little Big Horn.

The last idiosyncratic throes of modernism. Le Corbusier on a
bad day and Monsieur Le Corbusier had, I believe, several bad days.
Or maybe the workers forgot to put the windows in.
They were distracted, they were in love, or they just weren't
very good at doing their job.

In any case they had crossed into North Dakota before anyone had
taken stock. Gentlemen, there's a great deal of brick, six floors of it,
but no windows. Zany, cool even, and so liberal –
a Liberal Arts Building without the dictatorship of light!
I'm going to freak out and write a paper on Paul de Man.

Boom Boom Boom Boom I'm gonna to shoot you right down, right off your feet . . .

I feel like Louis Theroux. He's talking to a serial murderer in a prison cage who's shaved and full of tattoos. He has strangled several women with astonishing brutality but has recently found God even if God wasn't doing much to be found. How many more years have you got? I reckon I've got about 300 years. Gosh, that's quite a lot, says Louis and in the silence that follows you wonder whether the born again serial murderer might put his arm through the bars and grab the Englishman by the throat if only to knock the blankness off his face.

I'm talking to Professor Schnabel who has spent thirty years teaching Romantic Literature. What's it like, I ask, teaching Keats in a building without light? It's a figure of speech says the professor and life would be intolerable without figures of speech.
Free range Tom Turkeys and their sassy paramours wobble around the campus drunk on light and happy with the knowledge they will never have to write an essay on *The Great Gatsby* or *The Infernal Desire Machines of Dr Hoffman*.
And they don't give a coyote for the Futurist Manifesto – our speed, they say, is perfect as they bustle towards the statue of Crazy Horse. Sometimes they wonder what happens in the building without light and shudder.

One of the turkeys has a guitar, the others gather round, he's singing the Turkey Blues.
Up in the mountains there are bears and elk and moose and wolves and trees dripping with snow.

Boom Boom Boom Boom I'm gonna to shoot you right down, right
off your feet, take you home with me and put you in my house –
And in my house, sings some teenage joker, *there are windows*
throughout!

And they keel over with laughter, some of them are actually weeping.

I'm talking to the sisters – identical twins – professors of linguistics
and they're all ginsenged up. Who needs light when you're blessed
with the inner light? I'm Miss Mood, says the one with dark framed
spectacles and I'm Miss Lexicon says the other
whose spectacles are as dark framed as her sister's – perfectly
              interchangeable I guess.

Have you seen the turkeys? Yes. Have you, by chance, noticed
the window situation? Yes. They nudge each other. He's one smart cookie,
and then they laugh. We all laugh. When there was a quake in Oklahoma,
they tell me, the building without windows moved.

I reckon, Miss Lexicon says, the guy who designed the building also
designed Correctional Facilities and the Dean that year was having
some kind of spiritual crisis – and it was cheaper without windows
in any case, and no sign the war in Vietnam was finishing any time soon.

Maybe it had something to do with redemption.
It's not a metaphor, it's a pedagogical nightmare and we've been given
life sentences. It's like *Bleak House* but much longer and much bleaker,
no canaries released from any cages.

Oh hell, I say.

Miss Mood says that might be true but she has another theory,
however she's got a class so will have to tell me later.
See you later alligator. In a while crocodile.

When I'm alone in the Alumni House lying on a bed that could sleep
half the football team watching *Buck Off Special* at the Billings Bull
    Riding
Spring Testicle Buck Off Festival

I hear a voice in my head which insists on being listened to.
And one day
        Boom Boom Boom Boom
                I'm going to write it all down.

The Crucible

I dream of being that snooker player whose opponent
is so masterful there's nothing doing but to sit alone
in one's sartorial splendour occasionally sipping a glass of water
knowing that the camera is zooming in to investigate
your existential gloom, listening to the click of ball on ball
and the ripple of applause which accompanies your opponent's
unassailable lead. One needs to look the part, in defeat
as well as victory, certain that the pundits are making sly remarks
or even revealing a sudden sympathy for your spluttering career,
one of the best dressed players on the circuit, they're thinking,
yet one of the least successful.

You realise that you're actually fond of the sitting position,
a ring side view is not without advantages:
you find yourself remembering a wind in the trees and somewhere
there's a beach and the black sliding into its pocket is perfection,
even a kind of death. You're unexpectedly happy and you want
to hug your opponent, not just shake his hand; you want to hug him
like a brother, like a friend, like a lover, and the coloured balls
remind you of a Mexican Fiesta even though they've long slunk off
into the undergrowth. You feel like Siegfried or a workman
who's finished his shift at last – the sitting shift – who can now
lie down and relax and drink something stronger than water.

In fact you can't wait to kick off your shoes and the table is like
a manicured lawn – Please Keep Off – but now that you've lost
so stylishly, so effortlessly, you're going to lie down
on the grass, certain they will forgive you this indulgence,
given that you've spent so much time banished from the garden.
You can hang yourself with a tie but a bow-tie is like a fig leaf

which covers up your shame and because you've suffered such
a staggering defeat you're going to take it off and that's just the start.
You remember the wind and the beach and you're running free,
a trail of clothes behind you – naked, blissful, snookered.

I Can Feel You

Call the mole-catcher. He's dead.
Oh good. I mean good for the moles.
The whole of this side of England
is trembling. Veronica has a theory:
They're Dutch moles, they're good
at digging, the last time they came
was 1688, the Glorious Revolution
of the Moles. Do you remember?
There'll be windmills everywhere
and we'll have to eat that awful cheese
and clean the road outside our house.
And, says Cherry, speak a language
which absolutely nobody can understand.
We'll get used to it, says Veronica
and I do like an open sandwich.
And the Dutch are very tall. She's looking up.

She ought to be looking down:
mole hills, moles, unending voluptuousness.
Not a mole-catcher in the whole of
East Anglia. Either they've gone mad
or been carted off to Bletchley Park.

You thought the war was over –
that's what they call trick photography.
The war's still on! Round up the mole-catchers
and let moles have a prolonged period of ecstasy.

I'm lying on my mother's lawn,
hijacked by mole heaps.

Oh moles I can hear you
under the ground, reading extracts
from *The Monk* by Matthew Lewis
and doing a little free-style rap.

I can feel you, I can feel you.
I'm lying still looking at the sky.
Is that a Spitfire or an oyster-catcher?
Is it neither one nor the other?
Oh moles, I can feel you.

I can feel you.

Heat Wave

2018

My body is a text, I like to illustrate.
I thought your body was a body.
I can give you paper if you like.
My body is a manuscript of medieval vellum.
I am a walking palimpsest, a hermeneutic
cabaret. I'm available for close readings.
How closely would you like to be read?
If I revealed all you might have an epiphany.
Oh one of those, I said, they seem to be
occurring all over London.
No one loves a thin Falstaff, he said.

And football isn't coming home, Football said.

Charles Boyle Baudelaire is throwing a party
in Shepherd's Bush and I'm talking to a taxi driver
from the Horn of Africa.
(I rather like saying the Horn of Africa.)
The driver who is Somalian is complaining
about the heat.
In Mogadishu we have exquisite breezes.
I doubt we'll have many in Shepherd's Bush.

Christopher is lying on a sofa
in the cool of the house.
I was about to faint, he says –
we're all about to faint, I say, there, look, we've fainted!
Water, water, a glass of cordial perhaps?

A lady in white holds an oriental parasol
in the garden and leans forward
to wipe the face of Henry James Horovitz.

I'm talking to a Spanish poet who can't hear.
We get two beer cans and a piece of string
and she stands on one side of the garden
and I stand on the other.

Can you hear me now? I ask.
Nada, she says, absolutely fucking nada.

Boxing Day

The dogs are going crazy.
I think mother slipped them
some amphetamines.

A truly enormous ham
is being cooked

and the dogs are becoming idiotic and psychotic.

My ex-wife is late which is good
and not so good. Mother pulsates.

Welcome ex-wife, have some ham.
I watch Mother slicing slicing slicing.
Two pieces of ham for ex-wife,
and three pieces of ham for me.

O Bethlehem!
        O Bethlehem!

In England we eat boiled ham, Mother says.
Do you like boiled ham? Mother asks ex-wife.
Ex-wife says, I have been to West Ham,
I may have taken the wrong line.

After the enormous ham
Mother shouts, Pudding!
and off she walks to the special shed.

I am left with ex-wife.

Shall we dance? No.

Water has flowed under the bridge,
says ex-wife. Not enough I'm thinking.

Flee whilst you can, ex-wife! Flee!

Mother's walking back to the house,
the dogs have conked out
in some post-amphetamine afternoon lock-down.

Mother appears with a trifle.
An enormous trifle.
In England, Mother says, we eat trifle.

Trolley Man

When someone asks, Could I have
a sandwich with some cheese in it?
I will say No sandwiches today!

And if anyone should ask for coffee
I will say, Hot water not working.
Shocking, isn't it?

I will wheel my trolley from one end
of the train to the other, smiling
magnificently at everyone.

And when a lady asks,
I don't suppose you've got
a piece of shortbread
some lovely, lovely shortbread?

I will say, No my dear
all the lovely shortbread has gone.

Eau Sauvage
for Charles

Richard John Bingham, 7th Earl of Lucan (born 18 December 1934; presumed dead), commonly known as Lord Lucan, was a British peer suspected of murder who disappeared in 1974.

I get an unexpected
text from Lord Lucan:

Will you read my poems?
Yes, Lord Lucan, I will.

Tomorrow, when I look
for the message it isn't

there – I mean his part
of the message isn't there.

Just, Yes Lord Lucan I will.
It sounds like a song.

Yes, Lord Lucan, I will.
Yes, Lord Lucan, I will.

A week later a package
drops through the letter box –

22 Landguard Road
into a communal hallway,

full of envelopes
addressed to neighbours

who've long since disappeared:
Miss Moon, Miss Pinkerton

Miss Reckless, Miss Raven

and the loveliest of all
Miss Craven.

I read the poems
with trembling lips.

I read the poems
with trembling thighs.

I read the poems
with widening eyes

and then ring Charles Boyle
ex-poet of Shepherd's Bush.

Is that Charles Boyle
ex-poet of Shepherd's Bush?

Yes, says Charles
as – indeed – you well know.

I want to find the right *ton*

I want to suggest
that in a previous life

I rubbed shoulders
with interesting people.

A little hushed, throaty, I say,
The poems of Lucan have landed.

What are you talking about?
says Charles, are you demented?

I think you should take a look.
I think you should publish the book.

Actually, I rather enjoy thinking
of Charles Boyle in Shepherd's Bush.

Charles says, Read me a couple,
read me a poem by Lucky Lord Lookey.

Read me, read me. Alright, alright.
I'm sifting through the poems

and the room is zinging with
the aroma of Eau Sauvage.

Read me a couple, read me a couple.

I'm reading them to myself.
I'm not reading them to Charles.

I'm reading them to myself.
They're so louche and so elegant

so decadent and so intelligent.
In fact they're not poems at all.

They're too good to be poems.
It's like putting one's hand in a glove.

It's like smoking a little Tina.
Bonjour little Tina. Bonjour.

They're not poems at all.

Poems which are better than poems
ought to be called something other

than poems. Read me a couple
says Charles, read me a couple of poems

that are better than poems.

Charles is making a strange noise
at the end of the phone.

I have the most extraordinary
non-poems in the world

and Charles is making a noise
at the end of the phone.

The ex-poet of Shepherd's Bush
the most insouciant publisher

in the city of London
the most audacious publisher

in the city of London
the most charming publisher

in the city of London
is making a strange noise

at the end of the phone.

Oh read me a couple.
Oh read me a couple.

No! No! No!
And then I pretend
someone's knocking

at the door.

In fact I go to the door
and start knocking on it

knock, knock, knock:
Charles, I say, someone's knocking

at the door – You'd better
answer it, he says.

I think he might be thinking
it's Lovely Lord Lucky.

Knock, knock, knocking
at the door.

Who's knock knock
knocking at the door?

Virginia Woolf

Miss Photo-Synthesis

Frederick Seidel

Charles Manson

Charles Boyle

Not even Charles
can be in two places
at the same time –

Professor Kiss

Miss Reckless

Arthur Rimbaud
with only one leg

Salvador Dalí

Lord Lucan

alleged killer of Nannies,

holding some
lead pipe and

a mediocre bottle
of vodka.

Oh Lord Lucan

is knocking at the door!
(Obviously he isn't,

I'm putting on a
show for Charles!)

Hang on a moment, I say
walking round the room

in a euphoric circle.
Hang on a moment, I say

walking round the room
in a euphoric circle.

Sweet Lord – sweet Lord
someone *is* knocking

at the door!

I mean someone
who is not me –

someone who is not me!

The jazz police are leaning
on my shoulders.

The Poetry Foundation
is going through my folders.

Blah, blah de blah
                    blah

Charles is making a strange noise
and someone's knocking at the door.

And I have seen enough
black and white films

to know that the person
in the shit – which happens to be me

(how did that happen?)

needs to be fleet of foot
and I would be happy

to flush the poems – I haven't
yet thought of another name –

for the poems other than *poems* –
down the lavatory:

the flusher is a spitter
rather than a flusher

the flusher is a spitter
rather than a

I called the plumber
a hundred times.

His name is Trevor.
Oh, he's subtle.

I called the plumber
a hundred times.
I know he's there

at the end of the phone
feigning a psychotic attack

in the back of his van.

You can stick your little pins
in that voodoo doll.

I cannot flush
the Lucan poems.

I cannot burn the Lucan poems
not a log in sight.

OPEN UP! OPEN UP!

Lord Lucky has written
his poems on exquisite

parchment and I realise now
I will have to eat them.

That's what they do in France
when the Gestapo comes

knocking on the
                    door.

The young woman who
everybody loves drinks

a glass of Beaujolais

and swallows the name
of the agent which slips down

her throat

and lies in the pit of her stomach.
We know the Gestapo

will not break her –
they will torture her

and they will kill her.
She will die, having

swallowed the name

of a very important agent.
She will save France.

They will not break her.
There will be a statue of her

in Rue Julien-Lacroix
Je ne regrette rien / everything.

I am now eating the poems
of Lord Lucan

what a pity he wrote so many!

The Gestapo are knocking
at the door

and I am eating the poems
of Lord Lucan.

Eat eat eat.

Eat eat eat.

And I say – in a muffled voice
I'm coming! I'm coming!

Give me some extra moments
Meine Herren

I'm just getting out of the shower!
As if.

I called the plumber
a hundred times.

Maybe I should pretend
I am merely a piece of paper

and rustle, rustle
or maybe I should just lie doggo

for a while –

I'M COMING! I'M COMING!

I don't want the Gestapo
to think I'm some

dirty, unwashed poet
floating on the Oh là là

of drug-fuelled auto-erotica

so I'm dabbing
my neck with Eau Sauvage

and slipping on
the silkiest of dressing gowns

as if I'd just been putting
the final touches to

Blithe Spirit.
Dabbing on a little Eau Sauvage.

Eat eat eat.

Eat eat eat.

I'm coming! I'm coming!

The Road to Bastardo

You can eat from any tree
but not the one which yields
the figs. We ate plentifully,
the juice running down our chins.
A car pulled up. *Questa la strada
per Bastardo?* Yes, yes, we said
and wandered back to Daria's car –

sweet now with figs
and she drove fast across Umbria –
I haven't killed anyone yet
and would like to keep it that way.

Vineyards. Olives. Dust.

Monte Fucking Falco she cries out.
Then adds, I want to make a risotto
and have a line of Carrara White
if there were such a thing
or Umbrian Crystal or Spoleto Blue.
How would you get that up your nose?

Elmo the dog is eating a chair: yum-yum

and the stars are out and someone's
on the tower, the Duke of what's his name,
the Duke of weird shit is dancing
the Thirteenth Century Templar Blues
with a goat. He's the strangest fellow:
with a clutch of letters from Othello

such a mover and shaker in the bordello
and what a way with the violoncello!
so bello, so bello, so bello . . .
He waters the flowers with limoncello:

so mellow, so rose of Jericho, so Pirandello.

Goodbye Blackbird

I had this ridiculous pang of nostalgia for Italian
bureaucracy so I got a cheap flight to Genoa and
then a taxi to the Municipal Hall in Corso Torino where,
with satisfaction, I joined a queue, a long queue.

I hadn't done this for twenty years but I recognised
several faces. I could see Serafina, somewhat older now.
Have you been here all this time? I asked. Oh Giulio, she said,
each time I get to the front they send me to the back,
it's like a game which never ends. *Un bel gioco dura poco,*
I said. How is the world outside? she asked. Have there been
any changes? Would you hold my hand a while?

Birth Certificates, Marriage Certificates, Residency
and Divorce Certificates and – along the corridor –
the nondescript Office of Death Certificates.

Should I get one now? Two pigeons with a single bean?
Are you dead already? asked the woman behind the screen.
You seem somewhat vertical for a corpse.
Not yet, I guess, I have a feeling that death's rather like a
blackbird. Really, she said, a blackbird, who would have thought!

I need a date and the cause of death – I'm not allowed to
leave it blank. That would be unconventional and probably
against the law. Well, you would be saving me time, or saving
someone else some time. In fact, you would be saving hours of time
which is a kindness in itself and I would never say a word to
anybody. Listen here, I have to sign it, and then stamp it with my
stamper. I see, the whole thing seems something of a nightmare,
                                                              I said.

Blackbirds hey! However you are simpatico and actually
I remember you. Inglese non? Yes, signora, I am English.
My son works in London, she said, he lives in Tooting.
Tooting! Almost certainly a cause for celebration, I said.

I suppose another Death Certificate in the world
won't change much. Exactly, you choose the date and cause
of death and I won't look. Promise? she said. I promise. You
write in the details and it will be a secret I carry to the grave –
You sound like a nineteenth century novel! I do like Dickens,
she said, I even read Bleak House in English. I saw it as a kind
of penance, like a hundred Hail Marys and a great deal more
Pater Nosters. Now she was putting in the date and I looked
away.

She smiled and took out her stamper and stamped it twice.
Grazie. Bella giornata, have a nice day, I said. And you too,
signor inglese. Let only beautiful things occur and keep
your eyes peeled. I waved to Serafina and stepped out
onto Corso Torino. The sun was shining, the birds
were singing and I walked to Bar Bliss and drank a Negroni.

Sopraelevata

We have taken the Sopraelevata, Eugenio hits
the accelerator, it's like a coronary bypass
through the city. We're driving past bedrooms,
cuttlefish, monuments, bridges –
Zena etherised on a post-industrial operating table:
Palazzo San Giorgio, Tower of Morchi, la Commenda di Pré
superannuated villas, the unforgiving labyrinth
Dino Campana psychotic in the back streets,
gin and tonic Don climbing into the pantheon
my young self weeping in some medieval doorway –
To the left of us the docks, the cranes, the sea
suppurating pullulating liners, oil tankers, refugees
and the light house, la lanterna, Ligurian tumescence.
We're driving through the gash of the city
unhealed wounds, the luxurious stigmata.
They beat the city black and blue and let it dangle on the cross.
My love, I think we're driving past a crucifixion!
Shipbuilders gone, chemical and steel plants gone
Cornigliano, old style sci-fi incinerator, closed –
spitting out gobs of toxicity. Ten minutes to reach the airport.
Non piangere! Non piangere!

Tenement Nights

You are my outer and my inner
my white-arsed sinner
my macaronic – macaroni dinner
my karaoke singer, that sudden glimmer
of quince trees and kumquat.
You are my west and east
Babette's Feast, the morning yeast
my north and south, my hole and mouth
my white fly, my chemical high
my overheated bliss, my Glasgow kiss
my bruises and excuses.
You are the passing ice cream van
the Zen gardens of Japan.
You are my transcendental spheres
those drooling éclairs.
You are my Cessnock, my Govan
my Ibrox, my Partick
you are my thistle, my thistle
my fine dining, my morning gristle.

Love

Those weeds on the tracks
in Bogliasco could be eaten
by a goat, should a goat
be arsed to clamber down the hill.

I want to call them yarrow
waiting quietly for the White Arrow –
yet they're purple, royal purple:

a little hoity for a weed
beloved of goats – daydreaming goats!

They are sovereign, growing
between the tracks, the drummer boys
of this quiet station.

Until the White Arrow hurtles through
and they swing to the left
or they swing to the right

as if they were being blasted
by an enormous hair dryer.

And when the train has shot past
they rattle furiously –
a kind of death-dance

or an act of flirtation:
as if to say to the goats on high
Come and eat us
lazy head-butting sweethearts

before we die.

from What Were You Thinking? (2016)

Jerry Hall Meets Salvador Dali

I flew to Paris at seventeen
and got talking to Jean-Paul
Sartre and Simone de Beauvoir
over coffee. I was happy
to meet them. The trouble is
I just can't write poems
when I'm happy.

Mother said, The Riviera
is the place to go.
I bought a pink bikini,
some high-heeled shoes
and walked myself along the beach.

I love cooking. I love gardening.
I keep chickens. Mick's an alley cat.
Happy, happy, mostly happy.

Salvador Dalí said
Why don't you run naked
through my sculpture garden?

Alakefic

I'm lying on a brown leather sofa
chatting to Mother on the phone.
Mother doesn't hear awfully well

but that doesn't stop her from talking.
Sometimes she says, What's that?
My mother likes the word 'ballistic'

as in I nearly went ballistic or Veronica
went ballistic or the Bude-Smiths went
ballistic. And she often says

'facetious': I hope you're not being . . .
And a lot of people have chips
on their shoulders which is bad

and woe betide mutton dressed as lamb
and the word 'log' turns up quite a lot.
I'm down to my last log, she says,

do you think I should ring Neville?
I would, I say, lighting a cigarette.
You're not smoking!? she says.

Of course not! I've given smoking up!
I can hear my mother frowning.
And then she says, The trouble

with Neville is that he's so alakefic.
You're right about that, I say,
blowing smoke into the air.

King's Cross

When I lived in King's Cross
I used to lie in bed and listen
to my bones melting. At first
I thought I was listening to Elgar
and then I thought I was listening
to the couple who'd moved
into the flat above and who were
getting to know each other better
and then I thought I was listening
to the music of the spheres.
I was listening to my bones melting.

Émigrés

Now that my neighbours
have retuned to Poland

with their gaggle of children
and Mrs Grabowski making

one last indiscriminate visit
to the communal washing line

I think of sheets, my very own,
hanging somewhere in Gdansk.

I'm Homesick for Being Homesick

It's time to dress up
in the clothes of the dead
Mother said
having spent the afternoon
making chicken stock.

I wore my father's yellow socks
and my brother's moleskin trousers
and lowered two feet into my
sister's husband's elongated
boots – the ones that marched back
from Moscow on their own.

I popped on a shirt worn by
an uncle who hanged himself
and I put into my pocket a couple of
linen handkerchiefs belonging
to the gamekeeper before he walked
over a cliff – and here's the hat which
sat so well on Jacob's head.

And the coat worn by Captain Catastrophe
before he keeled over
with an attack of charisma and don't forget
the scarf, my mother says, as she
drapes it around my neck.

It's chucking down.
Oh good! I gather the lurchers
the smooth-haired lurchers
and stride across the heath.

Horizontal

I'm sick of being an upright green bin
full of the crap you chuck in my mouth.
In any case I'm an adolescent green bin
and I write poetry so I need to spend
a great deal of my time in the horizontal
position. When the wind blows I let
myself get thrown around the provinces
emptying gunk on the sodden streets.
If I end up in some cul-de-sac I'm happy!
Il faut être absolument horizontal.

I blow around Southampton
which I pronounce in a French accent
to buzz things up. Sometimes I bump
into bins of a similar disposition schooled
in the Parnassian tradition and eager
to transgress. Sometimes I'm as terrified
as 76,000 new-born pups,
other times my tongue un-cleaves itself
and I'm uncontrollably scatological. Mother's
going mad calling in social workers
and ringing the police. I can't get enough

of this new-style horizontal vagabondaggio.
I will not be God's little donkey!
Once I blew as far as Paris and fell in
with a bunch of soldiers. Something happened.
Sometimes I fetch up in London – that gorgeous
godless city. For a while I lived in Camden
in a somewhat chaotic same-bin relationship.

When I got back to Southampton,
or rather *Southāmptòn*, Mother went ape shit.
She needs to modernise, she doesn't like it one bit
when I say God is one mighty hypocrite.

Never mind. Look at me now. The horizontal green bin
blowing off to Addis Ababa. *Voilà, voilà.*

Burlington Arcade

I'm being carried down
the Burlington Arcade
by beadles in top hats,
jewellers on both sides
holding out their hands
and wrapped in cashmere.
When people speak of
near-death experiences
they're always going through
tunnels, they're happy.
They're never going through
The Burlington Arcade.

Eric says, It's good
to see you wearing clothes
and I have to admit he's
wearing the most beautiful
trousers and I say, Eric
you're not supposed to be
in his poem. Get back
into your shop! I can see
a light at the end of the tunnel.
The Head Beadle's saying
'Burlington Gardens!'

Should I tip him?
Am I dead?
What happens next?

Hampshire

When you drive me
into Hampshire
it always seems
you're taking me to bed:

a king-sized bed
involving vast amounts
of goose feather!

When you drive me
into Hampshire
cows stand in the mist

and swans loop on the river.
Let's stop the car!
let's find a glade,

a cavalry of bluebells.
I'll make the crook
of my arm into a pillow.

The Eau de Parfum of Mrs Radcliffe

Imagine a castle defended by poets.
How easily we capitulated!
The first cannon ball was enough
to send us into a collective funk.
The American lesbian stood on the parapet
and yelled in a blood-curdling way
for a while.

Our enemies – who exactly were they? –
were unimpressed by their victory.
They made us stay at the castle
and write poems in praise of defeat.

Boxes of food are left outside
the kitchen door and more or less
we fend for ourselves, though
we have the use of a cook called Hemingway
and Mary the housekeeper whose
Midlothian vowels make the animals
                                        twitch.

Sometimes some middle-ranking officer
dines with us, bringing some decent wine
and the cook conjures up
something reasonable and we have
to read our poems of subjugation.
The man with the stripe down his leg
leans back in the baronial chair with
a quixotic look, smoking an acrid cigar.

When they lock the narrow door
and all attempts to make thistle wine
dwindle into catatonic listlessness
we retire to our rooms to compose.

I had not realised how much
one could look at a tree and hate it.

The lesbian poet sobs.
Apart from the housekeeper
and Mrs Radcliffe
there are only men here:

she must be lonely –

Week after week:
a castle of poets crushed,
occupied, abandoned.
humiliated. Does humiliation
breed a special kind of love?

Poets disappear –
dragged off to a freak show
or lined up against the courtyard wall
and shot, their poems,
according to the commissar
guilty of a jouissance
which creeps into the writing
notwithstanding everything.

We pass round
the lugubrious cordial
willing our poems
to sink deeper

and deeper

and

For a while
there were six of us
but the middle-aged Italian
died of a broken heart
and the young poet
from Basingstoke threw
himself down a ravine.

A little more food
to go round and two
empty chairs –
could we use them for firewood?

Ah, the hour of tea.
Try some Verlaine!

My earnest neighbour
many a night
lets out a troubling wail,
his sleeplessness
is a kind of drug.

These sufferings
from other rooms
are what dreams
are made of.
He takes his solace
from the wildlife.

I have seen him
in the study
gazing rhapsodically
across the valley.
his book full of beautifully
written stanzas
in praise of the falcon,
his cheeks wet.

Oh danger, danger.

The castle creaks and groans
footsteps in the corridors,
a lavatory half-flushed,
a rattling key

and Mrs Radcliffe's
shockingly beautiful
Eau de Parfum.

One night I met the American poet
on the stairs by candlelight.

How much self-hate can there be? she asked.
I said, There can always be a little more.

And there's a poet called Jacob
who likes to wear a suit.
He's short and neat and taciturn
and is becoming balder by the day.
We never enter a poet's room
because that would be as if one were
putting a hand into the flame without
ever getting the chance of taking it out.

Last night Jacob knocked on my door
(he looked so small!) and thrust a poem
at me. Oh my heart was beating!
It was magnificent, and it was horrible:
such sensuous tropes, such ardour,
such languor, such candour, such . . .

I was envious that the muscles
of his heart were in perfect order.

He asked me to destroy it
and I put the poem in the sink
(oh look away!) and lit it
with a match.

When the rain went
and the sky cleared
and the sun shone

they sent a boy
to cut the grass –
a lovely boy!

He had a machine
which he rode across the fields
followed by a dog.

For a day the castle smelt
of cut grass, our hearts were giddy.

Such fragrance, such hope.
Let's put a stop to that!

Hemingway
took a pistol to his head
and shot himself
but the pistol was empty
thank goodness for that:
more soup, more boiled ham.
One day he pulled a trout
from the river.

The only time he smiled
was when he proposed
a round of Scottish roulette
a game which involves
a vast amount of porridge.
I really can't say anymore.

The days are getting longer.
Light through the valley.
Badgers bumping into badgers.

Jacob's dark suit
has become a raven
he flies to the wood,

a gift!

A bagpipe in the turret.
Did you hear it? A wound?
A warning? Nothing.

The man with the stripe
down his leg
doesn't come anymore.
Our poems bored him.
Our poems bore us.

Shall we write a poem
to the longest day?

Oh let's not!

There's drumbeat
in the hills, and gunfire.

Are they planning
to lay siege to the castle again?

A castle defended
by three poets
a housekeeper,
Mrs Radcliffe
and a neurasthenic cook.

Who will stand
in front of the cannon ball?

Who will win the poetry prize?

I think the housekeeper
has turned into a sparrow.
Look, there she goes!

I think Hemingway
has turned into a fish.
Let's put him in the river.

Have you thought
how quiet the castle is?
Birdsong, stag leap, wild flowers.

I think the soldiers have gone.
I think the soldiers were never here.

Gracious lesbian, honest rhapsodist
stop writing and be of good cheer.

The door is open
and there's a long drive
in which anything could happen
and at the end of the drive
there are gates, which
even as we speak, are opening.

Shall we walk along it?

Closed

The next station is Closed
which is exactly where I want to be:
it takes a while to get out
but eventually I find a bus
called Not In Service:
it's on the other side of the river
property is cheap
and there are Pleasure Gardens
which nobody visits
and a Bed and Breakfast called
No Vacancies (perfect!).
There's an ATM which never works
and a kebab shop.
A lot of people are cross-eyed
and the Protestant Work Ethic
is a weird sex club
which I'd recommend, mostly.

La Douceur de la Nuit

The refuse collectors
have been on strike for weeks.
I've never been so happy.

Bins have learnt to move
their hips. I've seen them
throbbing in the moonlight.

Have you heard
Cesária Évora's mournful song
to uncollected bins?

The rats link arms
and dance with melancholy
and the cats

have turned themselves
into aromatic troubadours.
When I open the windows

pungent fruit leaps
onto my bed and the black sacks
sway like belly palms.

Stations of the Cross

Someone has taken an axe
to my life which meant
that although everything
was in pieces we needed
a Christmas tree
if only for the children
to gather round as they listened
to a wound-up version of
Stille Nacht, heilige Nacht.

Someone had taken an axe
to the forest – now there were
Christmas trees throughout the city.
Lucky me! I took myself
to the Mercato Orientale
to pick up my tree
and screw down the thorns
because someone had
taken an axe to my life.

I picked up the Christmas tree
and carried it all the way
to our house on the hill
which had turned into
an outpost of hell
but even hell needs a tree
UN ALBERO DI NATALE.

I carried my tree
past the Hotel Metropoli,

I carried my tree
to Saint Anna's Funicular.
Oh, they said
it's Julian the leper
Julian of the *mot juste*
Julian with an axe in his head
carrying a Christmas tree
to an outpost of hell.

Sometimes people swung
a punch
just for the hell of it.
Someone started hammering
a nail into my head
just for the hell of it.
Evidently
I had done something wrong!
Then I carried my tree
along Corso Magenta
where the blind man
turned a blind eye.

And I carried my tree
up Salità Santa Maria della Sanità
and I carried my tree to the eight floor
because the lift was broken
and the woman who'd taken an axe
to my life said Ah un albero di natale,
we've been waiting so fucking long
for un albero di natale.

Put it there in the corner.
Careful, careful.
Oh look it's beautiful,
a little red perhaps
but nevertheless beautiful.
Here's a cloth
to wipe your face.
You'll frighten the children.
They'll think you've gone completely mad.

Via Monte Bello

The lampshade
hanging from

the ceiling
is Eleanor

of Aquitaine
kneeling

La Baia di Silenzio

I lay myself down
in the Bay of Silence.
The wind kicked up
and scudded across
the sea. The wind
got into the rigging
and the Bay of Silence
wasn't silent at all
with sails flapping
like scarecrows
on the threshold of
delirium. A girl
shrieked. Something
was coming off
the sea which
could only be death
or the sister of death
or the cocktail of
death or the methadone
of death or the
ecstasy of death
or the aftershave
of death or the sweet
morning feeling
of death, or the hit me,
hit me, hit me
of death, or the *la la la*
of death. Goodbye.

Minestrone

When I telephone
my erstwhile innamorata
she speaks in the voice
of minestrone. Not the minestrone
her mother would make
having stood the entire morning
in a small windowless kitchen
throwing diced vegetables
into a pot whilst intoning
Giacomo Leopardi's
The Approach of Death
.

No, it is not that voice.
Nor does the voice say:
I could rustle up a scallopina,
some grilled aubergines
and a salad so fresh and delectable
you would glow, *mio caro*, you would glow!

No, the voice is the voice
of a minestrone hunkering down
at the bottom of the pot:
it's thick and beginning to congeal
it will probably do for another day.

I could warm it up, *mio caro bello*,
and scrape it out with a spoon
and serve it to you in a bowl
whose hair-line crack has formed
two distinct geographical kingdoms.

I could do all of this for you
because once upon a time
do you remember? – you were my husband.

The Necropolis

When I walked into the necropolis
in Genoa I saw that every grave

had been allocated a panettone
and because the Council was in

broad terms a coalition of the left
every panettone was in a red box

and because every panettone
was in a red box I had a hunch

the old Maoist-Leninist-Stalinist
front were calling a meeting

with the dead and because the
dead were bored of being dead

they clapped and shouted
like nuns who have discovered

the libido and because nuns
have discovered the libido

I'm going to bring the poem
to a sudden end. Sleep well!

Napoli

The boat was beating across the bay,
we had our backs to Vesuvius,
the wind smacked our faces.
Naples was an enormous packet of cigarettes
you could smoke until you conked out:
the cigarettes were never going to run out
and nor was the coffee, the drugs,
the prostitutes, the locked churches,
the scooters, the rice cakes, the evil eye,
the boys called Gennaro, the funiculars,
the shrines to Madonna, the shrines
to Maradona, the bullet holes, the heat,
the permanent state of crucifixion.
Anyone could be crucified two thousand
years ago but to be crucified now,
to be crucified in Napoli – oh lift me up!

Lunch with Fleur

Somewhere in the freezer
Fleur had put a quiche.
Bought it for a street party
but it'd rained and, in any case,
what a shame to give it up.

The quiche climbed into the freezer.
It sort of liked it: its parts becoming one,
a flying saucer, a frisbee, in East Finchley.

It was a stroke of genius
to pull it out and watch it twitch
In the kitchen
rediscovering its pseudo-Gallic whatnot,
its thawing into chanson.
Quiche, you are my *chanson d'amour*:
small but perfect.

Have another piece Fleur said.
Have another *chanson d'amour*.
Let's sing I said, we could sing a duet.
I am tone deaf, I am a catastrophe
when it comes to duets
but there is something about the quiche
which makes me want to sing
and I want to dance the tango.

The quiche isn't a *chanson d'amour*
it's a tango by Astor Piazzolla
it's oblivion, total oblivion
it's the back streets of Buenos Aires.
It's late afternoon, quiche, quiche are you ready?

Buddhism

After years of silence
my ex-wife sends me
a salami through the post.

I have to sign for it
and then I take it
into the flat and put it

in the fridge. And then I remember
a Calabrian neighbour
who hung his salamis

in every room in the house.
He was a doctor, or had at least
acquired some kind of

medical qualification –
but no luck finding a job.
He practised Buddhism

and this endowed him
with patience and good feelings
especially towards the salamis

which, it has to be said, gave
the apartment a particular aroma.
I like to keep my hand in,

he said. And he took out
a knife and began to chop the salami
in the hallway. I take my ex-wife's

salami out of the fridge and spend
much of the day looking at it.
Years of silence and then a salami!

And I look for a sharp knife
and slice off a piece which,
a little nervously, I eat. Delicious.

Supper in Lorsica

Fiona says, Shall we take these home?
I have to say I'm not exactly drooling.

She plucks them out of the earth
and walks towards the flames like Joan of Arc.

When we get back to the village
Signora Volpone leans out of the window:

Avete trovato I funghi?
Fiona holds up the yellowy things:

Careful, careful, says Signora Volpone,
they might be the eyes of the devil!

She sends down her son who is bare-chested
and good at everything.

He looks at the mushrooms and smells them
and then he waves his much-waved Italian finger.

Don't eat them, he says.
Thank God for that, I'm thinking

And Fiona hurls them off the cliff.

Happy Carp Christmas
Prague

Usually you buy it
a couple of days
before Christmas
and throw it in the bath.
The children
give it a name
something like Marek the carp
and spend hours in the bathroom
falling head over heels
in love with it.
Then father kills it.

No one wants
to eat it,
especially the children.
It tastes of shit:
we call it the bottom eater.
No presents till
you've eaten your carp!

Everybody's shouting.
It's full of tiny bones
which get stuck
in the throat.
Some people choke to death.

Happy Carp Christmas
to everyone!
Happy Crap Christmas
to everyone!

Bohemian Horseradish

For the first time in my life I pre-order
a taxi to pick me up at the airport.
I'm going to Prague. The taxi will cost 650 crowns.
I'm almost certain my internet exertions
will result in nothing. There is a reference number
which I remember to write on a slip of paper
and which I lose immediately. I'm rather
hoping there won't be anyone at the airport
holding up a piece of paper with my name on it.
I'm enjoying the idea of getting the wrong tram
and slipping into the heart of nowhere.

So imagine my surprise when I walk out
of the airport and see among the throng
of names one which says MR STANDARD.
I am the visitor they anticipated; he will want
some Czech beer, a trip down the river
and some Roasted Pork Knee with a little
Bohemian Horseradish and he'll want to stand
on Charles Bridge with an arrow in his head.

A man with a scraggy beard and a beige jacket
and smelling of cigarettes clasps my hand –
Welcome to Prague Mr Standard, my name is Peter.
I will drive you to the Hotel Magnificent.

Smoking in my car is acceptable he says
throwing out a butt-end with extravagance.
What do you do? he asks. I teach.
I had a Russian girlfriend with a diploma

in Shakespeare; no one could understand her,
not even Shakespeare! A joke, yes. I guess
she was very clever, I say. She was useless
at everything – a blonde with big boobs.
He takes his hands off the steering wheel
to show how big they were. I bought her T-shirt
which said I AM THE BLONDE – SORRY.
She went back to Moscow.

Bloody shit, he says, you talk so much I lose
the road, never mind I show you short cut –
He drives through a tunnel and then shoots
across a yap of land and re-joins the motorway.

Your English is very good, I say. Thank you.
I lived in Lewisham for two years.
I didn't need a diploma in Shakespeare!
Have another cigarette. Thank you.

The Hotel Magnificent is in a bad zone
full of gypsies who will take your
money, your trousers and your nose –
I'm thinking of Roasted English Nose
on a bed of Bohemian Horseradish.
And then as if he had a gift for discarding
last things he pulls off his nose, lowers
the window and chucks it out.
Double Portion of Roasted Nose
on a Bed of Bohemian . . .

I could take you to the Hotel Fantastic
where everything is top shit and
you could sleep in peace listening to Dvořák
of the trams with your nose in harmony.
Choice is despair, I say, and in any case Peter
I booked a room at the Hotel Magnificent.
I'll take my chances. Oh Mr Standard, he says
(tapping his nose), I'm now wondering
if I haven't by mistake picked up the wrong man.
He leaves me at the Hotel Magnificent.
I pay him 650 crowns and he gives me a receipt.
He says, I like talking to you, my name is Peter.
If you want anything this is my number:
blondes, diplomas, boys, drugs – my name is Peter.
I lived in Lewisham for two years.
I check in, lie on a bed, and listen to the trams.

Next day I'm sitting in a scruffy park
full of dog shit, smoking a cigarette.
A young man – unmistakeably a gypsy –
is pushing a baby towards me. I feel a twinge
at the end of my nose. When he gets to the bench
he stops and says something. I shrug.
The boy starts shouting and walks towards a bush
leaving the baby next to me.
When I look at the baby again it seems odd,
I'm wondering whether it's a stuffed baby.
It doesn't appear to have a nose.
The boy is having a slash in the bush,

it seems to be a very long slash and I notice
the park is full of gypsies with stuffed babies
(if, that is, they are stuffed). Oh Peter
I should have gone to the Hotel Fantastic.
Even now I could be listening to Dvořák.
I can smell the hot dogs from the hot dog stand.
How much longer will I be able to smell them?

The Gargantuan Muffin Beauty Contest

We were at the Edison Hotel on West 47th Street
for the annual muffin beauty contest –
I can't tell you how pumped up we were.
Times Square was having another psychotic judder.
The bellhop was all thumbs up: Sir, have a nice day
and get one gratis. All those avenues of doors
and the Hispanic chambermaid who couldn't speak English.
Spider-Man was doing all that Spider-Man shit
to get a bird's-eye view. Donna Summer
was almost dead and we were barely into spring.
I want to dance to Love to Love You Baby, I want to groan.
I've never seen so many high-quality muffins.
If I wasn't a religious man, and maybe I wasn't
I would have said the muffins were walking on water.
I've never felt so half and half. Have you read the Bible?
The bellhop said You ain't seen muffin yet.
They were drifting in from Queens, Brooklyn, Harlem,
the Bronx, Manhattan muffins too and that weird
cute coke-faced muffin who'd taken the subway
from Coney Island. If only I were a betting man,
but hey I am a betting man, it's Coney Island every time.
Lou Reed isn't getting any younger. Zappa said:
Girl you thought he was a man but he was a muffin,
he hung around till you found he didn't know nuthin.
In the lobby Nina Simone was singing, I loves you Muffin
and in the restroom they piped in Mack the Knife:
Hey Sookie Taudry, Jenny Diver, Polly Peachum
and old Miss Lulu Brown. *Muffin The Romance*
was the biggest show in town. We were hurtling back
to the 1970s and sometimes the 1970s are almost

as good as the 1930s. I want my muffins to be ahistorical:
hallelujah, to say ahistorical makes me joyful.
I saw Leonard Cohen crooning with a couple
of octogenarian muffins and I'm telling you now
the lobby was pleasantly disturbing. You may find
yourself behind the wheel of a large automobile.
You may find yourself in another part of the world.
You may find yourself at the gargantuan muffin beauty contest
and you may ask yourself, Well, how did I get here?
Times Square was having another psychotic judder.
Love is in the air, in the whisper of the trees.
This is not America, this is the cover version:
Sun, sex, sin, divine intervention, death and destruction,
welcome to *The Sodom and Gomorrah Show.*
All those white muffins trying to be black muffins!
Give us our daily muffin, save us from temptation.
Jimmy Buffet was singing, Why don't we get drunk
and make out? In Times Square the most beautiful muffins
in the world were hanging on a thousand screens.

Dinner with Val

Val was saying, I just got messages through
and put them in a box and at the end of the war
they gave me a medal. No idea what happened to it.
And when the pilots were floating in the sky
it was exhilarating and we raced across the fields
hoping the men would be okay and hoping
for a bit of parachute. Some of the Germans
were charming, such a shame they were German.

Parachute pants were the thing and Veronica
actually got married in a parachute, mind you
she was marrying a pilot – a lovely man –
even though he'd lost a leg which,
I suppose, made some things awkward.
And then I worked in the War Office pushing
planes and ships around with a stick and
on one occasion Winston came in with a dog.

A black dog, and if I'm not mistaken
it had a funny eye – Oh dear should I have said that?
Winston said, Do carry one and goodness how we did.
I saw a ship lurking around off Scotland and
shoved it into the Pacific – that whizzed things up.

I got another medal for that.

The Recipe
for Toby

All I could remember
about the recipe was
that you had to separate
the eggs, as if the eggs
had a pathological dislike
for each other, or maybe,
like teenage kids, they just
egged each other on,
or maybe they were bad:
I put one in the pantry
and the other in the small
room along the corridor
and I said to myself,
not without a feeling of
triumph: I have separated
       the eggs.

East Finchley

It's always sunny in East Finchley.
It's always funny in East Finchley.
That's enough about East Finchley.

from The Parrots of Villa Gruber
Discover Lapis Lazuli (2011)

The Blessing of the Octopus at Lerici

Ever since the octopus raised itself
above the water and threw its tentacles
around the church bell and heaved it
this way and that way in order to tell us
the corsairs were coming to plunder
we have continued to bless the octopus.

That hasn't stopped us from eating it.
After all eating is a kind of blessing
and the priest who hasn't quite managed
to get the sand out of his shoes and
who comes from good peasant stock
throws on a green-braided jacket
and treks down to the gathered boats.

In truth he'd rather be tucking into
a plate of clams or a magnificent chop
than fooling around with an octopus
but he's got his psalter and he's learnt
a few lines form the poet Sbarbaro.

Water's sprinkled and there are chants
and the octopus raises itself from
under the sea and wraps its tentacles
around the poet-priest and pulls him
down to the weeds where psalters slip,
where jackets bloom. There's sunlight
on the surface of the water: the priest
is cuttlefish and the priest is bone.

Caffè Degli Specchi

What I want now is a little Vivaldi
which is terribly *infra dig* in some quarters.
But sitting here in the Café of Mirrors
where I've been sitting for twenty-five years
drinking a pale version of Green Tea
delicately fused with ceramic blue
a Vivaldian quick step might do the trick.
It would be so much better than the song
coming from the radio which has something
to do with a bell and the exhortation
to ring it and to ring it and failing that
to lie down on the floor and shudder.
If Vivaldi is no longer available or too *infra dig*
a little slow jazz or even a little low jazz
would capture the mood of the city
not to mention the mood of this Green-Blue Tea
which is holding up the sweetness of my tart.
And whilst I've been talking to you
distracting you from the drumbeat of the heart
so many things have happened:
the mirrors are gleaming and the girl with the cloth
has created a new world order
and the boy, rather beautiful, with his *cioccolata calda*
is lowering a brioche into the dark soup.

Plan B

We're trundling down Via Balbi
past palaces of glory and endless virtue.

We're fecund with children, we're good at that
and some of us have rabbits in our pockets.

We're fluent in dialects,
and we're making our way to Caricamento

to catch a steamer for America.
The crossing will not be pleasant.

We'll be sleeping cheek by jowl, cheek to cheek –
the air so foetid.

When we get to Ellis Island
some of us will be tested for lunacy.

How many legs does a dog have?
Who is the president of the United States?

The Parrots of Villa Gruber Discover Lapis Lazuli

We had spent so much time thinking about this moment
that we took on a flat at the very top of a very tall building

which had a stairway that led you to a precarious look-out.
The view of the sea! Some days I thought I'd turned into Zeus.

We rented the flat, a flat which was quite impractical, because
its corridors led into rooms and out again into more corridors,

the floors were wooden and the ceilings were as high as cupolas.
When the sun shone, which was often, we were drenched in light

and sometime the most unlikely parrots landed on the windowsill.
I even wondered if it might be wrong to live in such a dazzling world.

Sometimes I came home with a bottle of Dolcetto
and we sent the children to a friend who was kind to them

and we looked at each other and thought Yes, it could happen soon.
And it did. I can't recall exactly what the music was

but it was a music which allowed us to take off our shoes and stockings
and dance and dance and dance down this corridor and through that room

and down yet more corridors and along exquisite, derelict floors.
It is this, years later, even if you would have given Pontius Pilate himself

a run for his money, and even though, and how I shrank at the thought,
you dragged my name this way and that way through the Palace of Justice

and even though you built a moat around everything I loved –
the things I could tell you about those journeys in the dark,
    my hand on the tiller!

the parrots in their colourless sleep in the careless gardens of the Villa –
It is this I remember and sometimes I think of reaching for a glass
    and raising it to you.

Bruno Cuts my Hair in a Place Called Ether

Never to walk in Piazza Marsala
or cut through the Mercato Orientale
buying fillet steaks for little Jack.
Never to make a dish out of Zucchini flowers.
Never to walk down Salita Santa Caterina
or pass through the Galleria Mazzini.
Never to stand on the quayside of Genoa
with a suitcase full of straps and strings.
Never to take out a map of the world and say
I was there and there and there and there.
Never to tell the joke about the hot lemons.
Never to walk to Lavalu and see the dead
or take part in the great Ligurian lamentation
which is lupine recreation and catharsis.
Never to walk in The Street of Perfect Love
or rub Rina's back under dim-lit chandeliers.
Never to open the fridge and find a robin.
Never to hear the sirens, never to cook a rabbit.
Never to curse God, *Porco Dio! Porco Dio!*
Shave me Bruno, caress me with scissors.
Magnificent masseur, pull out thy electric hand.

My Beautiful Son Cooks me an Octopus

by hiring a boat in the fishing village of Camogli and heading off
for the waters of Zoagli. He has his hand on the tiller
and he's telling me that one day he's going to be a champion boxer.

He's taking me to Zoagli because he wants me to see the fish.
I don't tell him that when he was born the fish leapt clean out of the sea
nor do I tell him that when his mother was going nuts

the fish of Zoagli flew straight into my head and flapped.
I don't say If you could open my head and let the fish go free
I'd take the day off and pretend that life was sweet.

Villa Giovanna

Welcome to the Sailors Chapel and Reading Room
where there's an array of bibles
& evangelical currents are blowing down the corridor.
We could talk about the spirituality of seafaring
or we could lie down and sleep, our beds now still.
When I wake I'll put on those red slacks
& walk to Principe and then onto Via Balbi
where I'm sure to meet Signora Balbi:
Salve Signora Balbi, salve! Salve Giulio!
I'll step into the Faculty of Foreign Literature
& walk up to the loggia which is holding off the sun:
I'm going to talk at length with carissimo Sertoli
because he's turning into Marcello Mastroianni.
Look, he's getting out those lethal cigarettes.
But I've not smokèd for two whole years! he says
(now rather sadly putting them away). He pats my arm:
Giulio, I have a strategy & he takes out an elegant stick
of liquorice & begins to chew & he takes out another
which he hands to me and says, It's not so bad, is it?
not – mind you – as good as the camel
but something nevertheless to put into the mouth.
We are chewing liquorice on the loggia
casting into the past, our cloud of disbelief
& now when there's a hiatus in our liquorice talk
I notice a shadow throwing itself across the loggia
& see the illustrious Bacigalupo striding forwards,
an expert on Wallace Stevens, he too is wearing slacks!
Liquorice and comity. Elegance and intelligence.
Ho preso due piccioni con una fava!
I continue past the Church of Annunziata

next to the Liceo Classico where my son learnt Latin
but stumbled over Greek. And Via Lomellini, Via San Luca,
Piazza Banchi, Piazza Campetto (ah the shop that made
my wedding rings . . .) & the church of San Matteo,
church of christenings & bonbonniere.
The old lean priest is standing in the piazza.
Sin is beautiful, he says, sin has many gaudy wings
& without it I would be out of a job and he winks
placing a hand on my shoulder and pointing up
to The Miracle of the Ethiopian Dragons by Luca Cambiaso.
I push up through the Salita Archivescavato,
Migone the wine shop is there on the corner!
& onto the Questura in Piazza San Matteotti.
City of sweat and city of debt.
I'm looking at the left flank of the Doge's Palace
the white hips of the Doge's Palace
& I'm climbing the stairwell of denouncements
to greet that carabiniero who arrested me
for crimes in Villa Gruber.
It's hot now – *caldo, caldo, caldissimo.*
See how the sweat leaps from one onto the other
see how the ragazzi are wearing their occhiali scuri
the swinging cocks of the vicoli:
the Duomo and Via San Lorenzo. Left Bank of the city:
Salita Fava Greca, Piazza Sarzano. Oil tankers.
Via San Bernardo, kiff and marocchini:
my back to the tower, eyes seawards like Poisedon
why not ascend to San Nicolò, the quickened air beyond?
I take the funicular to Via Preve
& walk to Villa Giovanna.

I'm in the shower, the blue-tiled shower room
I'm scrubbing the sweat off myself
Oh listen! My liver's playing a little tune
& there's a white towel, almost a beatitude
& the city's turning into Havana with Scottish castles
& Ruth's on the terrace holding a melon.
I've never seen such a voluptuous thing!
Come, eat, she says, I have cooked.

What Did I Find on Bogliasco Beach

Bottle-tops, bottle-tops, bottle-tops
grey stones and some smaller red ones too

desiccated seaweed, *stuff mostly*
and something that once hung from a tree.

And oh yes I found a pair of lips.

Furthest, Fairest Things

Darkness has fallen
upon the Ligurian hills
and a warm breeze
blows across the terrace.

My hosts' hormonal daughters
enjoy another shower
and we gaze at the stars.

That, says Marco, is a mozzarella
and he's right –
the sky is full of them tonight.

Bocaccio speaks of this
and Chaucer makes recondite
allusions in the *Astrolabe*.

Look, says Marco, see how close it is!
We hold our breath
and watch the lovely thing
shoot low across the valley.

Later a mozzarella on our plates
daughters dressed and sweetly scented
we toast the mysteries of the sky.

Oliver

I'm in Lorsica,
there's not a cigarette in sight.

There's Oliver:
the most simpatico mongrel in Liguria.

He's small, he's white,
his eyes are popping out of his head.

I wish I could smoke him.

Late Swimming
Bogliasco

When I want to be near my brother
I walk inro the sea and swim breaststroke
so that my chest and stomach are
pointing down and I can feel his finger

scrape its way down my front which is
peculiar but homely and when
I've swum a sizeable distance
I tread water which feels like I'm sitting

on his shoulders which is wonderful
and then I know I must head back
because the boats are becoming
an archipelago of lights summoning

the fish into their nets, the very fish
that will beat a jig
on the marble slabs
when the city's clattering into life.

My brother holds my feet
and I can see the shore slipping
into the cocktail hour and I have
to speak to him, not unkindly.

Brother, it's good to be with you
and I'm glad you're doing well
but my time has not yet come
and people are waiting on the shore.

I feel his hands let go
which means I can really strike out now
and soon the shore is coming fast
and I don't look back.

The Seedy School of English

for Z

If I were to set up a school
I'd call it the Seedy School of English.
It'd be in some unspectacular Italian town
which already has the Oxford School
of English, the Regent School of English
and The Shining School of English.

One has a man with a bowler hat
and a caption – mistranslated perhaps –
A Hard Teacher is Good to Find.
Another shows a protruding tongue
emblazoned with the Union Jack.
Another reveals an emblematic oyster.
I'd put up a flickering neon light.

I can tell you The Seedy School of English
wouldn't be that big:
maybe two rooms, even one
and a reception area which would be perfect
for a girl called Rosalba.
One of the requirements of the job
would be a low level of English.

Not that Rosalba would appear very often:
partly because The Seedy School of English
wouldn't have much money
and partly because of a medical condition
which would prevent her from doing anything
other than getting pregnant.
I'd put up a picture

of a London taxi and a double-decker bus,
a map of the underground perhaps
and something with the Queen,
as well as a poster which said
When a Man is Tired of London
He is Tired of Life.

Riviera Blues

After she'd gone absolutely
mental in the Continental
I took Gloria to the Astoria.

Don't Die

My soul is humming along the Thames
is an ill-advised way of beginning a poem
unless you're Keats or overcome by
such a Keatsian swoon
which on a day like this near Pimlico
when you're strolling by the river
offering your heart to Lambeth Place
is not so difficult to believe.

I saw a lot of blood in the hospital.
I used to staunch the blood
and truth to say I was a specialist
when it came to blood. In fact it is
the word which rhymes most perfectly
with flood and on a day like this
near Vauxhall I'm waiting for the river's
gaudy ink to surge against the banks.

See me clutching arteries!
St Thom's, hospital of blood.
I cannot recognise it but that was where
the painful contract was beaten out
which served me well and served me ill:
pulse, poetry, pulmonary visions.

My soul hums along the Thames
and I'm drifting in and out of Fanny
is an ill-advised way of continuing a poem
unless you're dying or dead or feel
a magpie standing on your heart which

on a day like this on the banks of the river
when all that's left is a summer breeze
is not difficult to believe.

Under the surface of the Thames
the dead are blowing bubbles:
imagine phalanges of men and women
and children dressed in sartorial black
and so perfectly choreographed.
They want to sing but when they open
their lungs they send a volley
of bubbles to the world which cannot see them.

Portrait of Isabel Rawsthorne
Standing in a Street in Soho

Birth, and copulation, and death.
They're the facts when it comes to the brass tacks.
Birth and copulation and death

and a forest bleached with frost
and a sheep maybe, and a walk along the street
and going to the butcher's for a chop

and coming back with osso buco
and some tip-tap on the corner.
If it doesn't look easy you're not working hard enough.

And bumping into Isabel Rawsthorne
who's standing in a street in Soho
who doesn't look well somehow

who looks as if she's lost her keys
who looks as if she's lost her foot
who looks as if her face has gone completely AWOL.

Hi Isabel, I say, I've got a bag of osso buco.
I wanted to buy a chop or a little bacon
but I ended up with osso buco.

The Nightingale Sings in Bucharest

Imagine you have a whistle but no train
and you're standing on a small platform
outside Budapest and when I say Budapest
I was thinking of those years of dust
and why does the heart leap so in Bucharest?
When the map quivers
you find yourself consumed by one of Turin's
necromantic dreams.

In Warsaw the hotel overlooked the Ghetto –
a few sheds, the remains of a wall, a plaque.
It was difficult to breathe.

It matters because the platform
is a functioning slab and the warmth
of the city has gone. You know that
out there in the night is a train of people
you could have loved. Some were taken
by soldiers, some taken by the sea.
Some without any regard for originality
threw themselves out of windows.

Out there in the darkness a train of the dead
is hurtling in a fanfare of rectangular light.
In one of the carriages there's a samovar
and vodka is loosening up the corpses.
Neither can you see the train nor hear it
even if you strain like a dog on a leash.

You know the whistle's rhythm and the
the whistle's blood can pull the train
out of Ukraine and out of Deutschland and now
I've mentioned Ukraine is there a man here
who doesn't reach for a violin?
You're blowing this whistle in a European night –

through which a train of the almost-dead is hurtling
under the rule of vodka and hip-sway.
The train holds onto the note of the whistle
like a nightingale which has put itself back together:
wings, beak, heart, song.

A whistle, a whistle, oh see what you have done.

Bare Back

That rather distracting evening at Brigit's.
The garden's been neglected for years
and is beginning to move into the house.
Sometimes a bird flies into the room
knocks something over and flies into the night.

That's nature, Brigit says, which reminds her:
it was so hot I took all my clothes off
and got on the horse and rode bare back across the prairie.
Not a person in sight and, goodness, the vibrations.

I sent a piece to *The Lady*.
It was 1963 I believe. They published the whole thing
apart from the bit about the horse, which was a shame.
In any case I've written a poem about it
which I'm going to read to you very slowly.

Well-Regulated Dumplings
Munich

They're playing jazz in the Platz
which is cool because when you smile
the whole world wants a little Schnitzel.

They might be old and melancholic
but they're playing jazz in the Platz
which is cool because when you smile
the whole world wants a little Kunst.

They're playing jazz in the Platz
which is cool because they're making
little rooms in your head which
are so light and so free

that Ludwig One and Ludwig Two are going into the air
that the Rathaus mit Glockenspiel are going into the air

that the Blumen and Schweinenacken are going into the air
that there's been a sighting of Max Beckmann in the air

that the Englisher Garten are truly, truly gorgeous in the air
that Rudolf Steiner has become a special rocket

that well-regulated dumplings are going upwards
that buckets of cream are going, going into the air.

This is a lightness which is lighter than light,
this is a lightness which is lighter than skin
that I have to ask myself Is this death?

But why wrap yourself up in knots about a thing like that
because when you smile – *ja* – because
when you smile the whole world smiles with you.

Vonnegut's Dresden

The first fancy city I'd ever seen –
a city full of statues.
We were living in a slaughterhouse,
a nice new cement-block hog barn.

Mornings we worked in a malt syrup factory.
The syrup was for pregnant women.
The sirens would go off
and we'd hear some city getting it bad –
whump whump whump whump.

We thought we were safe.
There weren't any shelters in our town,
just clarinet factories.
Then the sirens went; February 13th, 1945.

We went down two stories
below the pavement into a meat locker.
It was cool there,
all those cadavers hanging around.
When we came up the city had gone.

Soup

Soup will keep us afloat.
Soup is our mainstay of hope.
That winter we bathed in it,
ate it, great pots of soup
full of beans and bones.
Mother, the farmer's daughter,
knew hearts were whittled
that feet were cold.
Mother, the soldier's wife,
knew the woodstove needed logs
that soup would shrive.
Soup is God's younger brother.
Soup is Corinthians.
Soup is patient, soup is kind.
It does not envy; it does not boast.

My mother gave me a pot of soup
made of beans and bones
that needed two strong arms
and a crack of the back
and I carried it to my sister
whose dogs have lupine thoughts
and although crows cawed
and deer scuttered
and the storm did that
Oh-the-storm-is-coming number
we drank our soup so that
our chins were wet with it
and when the dead came by
and I can tell you

there's been no shortage
of the dead in our house
they were heartened by the soup.
There was no stinting.

Oh soup keep us afloat.
Oh God's little brother
abide with me
in the kitchen of mother.

Scallops for Tracy

Steve's cooking scallops for Tracy.
He'll use a little too much cream.
The scallops won't resist that much.

Steve's cooking scallops for Tracy.
Everything bar the cooking's almost ready.
He's about to undress and step into the shower.

Tracy's slipping out of Darlington.
She doesn't know about the scallops.
She is unsure about her level of resistance.

Steve's scrubbing himself in the shower.
It's true he's put on a little weight.
Who wants to sleep with a will-of the-wisp?

Steve's cooking scallops for Tracy.
He needs to shave and apply some Eau Sauvage.
A man with scallops is a man who shaves.

Tracy is halfway along the motorway.
She's bought herself a nice little dress.
She's never in her life eaten a scallop.

Dog Talk

Why be adrift
when you could be a dog?

Why be a heaving breast
when you could be a dog?

Why take on a mortgage
when you could be a dog?

When take a trip to Nam
when you could be a dog?

Why be an Oxford Blue
when you could be a dog?

When be a blue stocking
when you could be a dog?

Why drool over a mozzarella
when you could be a dog?

Why stake your reputation
when you could be a dog?

Why do a Ph.D.
when you could be a dog?

Why pen a sonnet
when you could be a dog?

Why broker peace in the Middle East
when you could be a dog?

Why be a lunatic
when you could be a dog?

Why be twenty-third in line to the throne
and why be Home Secretary

and why be a triple jumper
when you could be a dog?

Why be a crock of shite
when you could be a dog?

Why go to the trouble of preparing a bong
when you could be a dog?

Why be the morning mist
when you could be a dog?

Why be a dog in the manger
When you could be *the* dog?

Why have two legs
when could you have four or even three?

Do You Have to Live in Paris to Be a Flâneur?

I'm walking down Shirley High Street.
Could someone come and get me now?

The Seabirds of Pimlico Hanker After Sapphires

I had a crazy idea we could have a good time:
you're flying in from Italy on Alitalia
and I'm booking a room in Edward Lear's old house
all sorted with my promiscuous credit card.
I take you to the Gay Hussar in Greek Street
where you can say anything you like
and because we're having a good time
I smile and offer you some Schnitzel.
Later, after I've paid the bill without flinching
we take a taxi to a discreet point on the Thames
where a boat is waiting full of elegant people.

It's a beautiful night and the orchestra seems
Welsh somehow. They're playing jazz
but they also throw in several Lieder. Everyone
looks good and so do you and, apparently, I do too
and before you know it we're dancing on the deck,
a little Cole Porter and some Bunky Green,
our luminous children are following the boat
like mermaids but in actual fact they're boys
with your looks and my intelligence but
I close my mouth because the captain of the boat

deserves to live, the orchestra deserves to live . . .
Our earthly boys are hauling themselves
onto the deck as if they were part of an advert
and they see their parents dancing cheek to cheek
and before you know it we're sitting round a table
and the waiter's bringing audacious cocktails.
It feels so good it feels like cocaine but it isn't.

It feels as if all the Carabineri and all the lawyers
are seabirds flying off to Pimlico and although
it would be foolish to talk of love
the whole of London's lit up like a beating heart.

England

for Mark

England is now called eat as much as you like.
Since the Beatles produced their first LP

England's hotter by a whole degree.
Olives, damn it, have been seen in Dorset.

England, England, you'd be crazy not to live there.

from The Red Zone (2007)

Mortlake
1982

Sometimes I gave Yiannis the slip.
I'd nip into the kitchen yard,
a hefty chop of jiving maggots,
smoke a Marlboro and relax.

I'd take a large brown egg from the fridge
watch it resting in my hand,
and hurl it high above the wall,
the road, the nearby station, Mortlake . . .

Sheep at Shingle Street

I did not come to write about sheep.
I came to feel the salt on my tongue.

It was the sheep which stayed with me.
Those quiet, humble, uncooked creatures.

That night I heard the sea,
saw sheep bobbing in the waves.

Piazza Della Posta Vecchia

Darling, they've dripped gold lights over our piazza,
the knocking shop of our glorious epoch
where the Borgia Prince Bettino Craxi
called by and hovered in the courtyard,
buoyed up by a team of squeaking puppets.
We peeped out naked, so sexually wired.
Come back to bed, you said.
That's when I noticed we didn't actually have a bed.

Vico San Marcellino

A small dish of fried fish.
Will you give me some?

The Red Zone

I need to get back to the Red Zone
because I left something in the apartment
ten, twenty, thirty years ago.
And this row of pants lining the alleyway
handwashed, sparkling.
I need to climb these slate stairs.
Has anyone bothered with the locks?
I thought the city so quiet
until helicopters drifted over my shoulder.
I need to get into that apartment
with its high ceilings, its whorey curtains,
the bat still flapping in the wardrobe,
a baby on the table.
Did someone leave a baby on the table?

Tripe

Do you remember the old Tripperia
in Vico Casana where you could shuffle along
on a cold winter morning
and eat a steaming hot plate of tripe soup?
Ah yes, I do, I do.

They brought in those new European regulations
which means they have to wipe the tables
at least once a month with some kind of damp cloth
and put in a special loo for the handicapped.
A special loo for the handicapped!
Exactly, as if someone with a handicap
would want to trundle down Vico Casana
to eat a steaming hot plate of tripe soup.

Well there you go, even if they did, they can't now.
The regulations were so complicated
they decided to shove the soup.
You can still get the tripe but no soup on the premises.

I see. Actually, I never cared much for the soup.

Riviera Night Train

The night train along the Riviera picked up pace:
windows open: we were airbrushed and buffeted.

I could smell the seabream out there in the water.
I had to mark a hundred papers before stepping down at Principe.

Sometimes the giddy scripts leapt into the night.

Barbera

I've got a bottle of Barbera but Lucia's out.
She must have a tire-bouchon, or something.

The bottle of Barbera is purple red
and I've got some pasta on the go.
I do want to open that bottle of Barbera.

The Moroccans don't have a tire-bouchon.
The Chinese won't open the door.
Should I try the people from Buenos Aires?

Dogs yap and spill onto the stairs.
An old woman stands on one side of the table.
Her son is holding open the door.

There's a bottle of Barbera on the table.
They smile when I explain why I am there.
They ask me in for a glass of Barbera.

The Poetic Revolution Begins Here

Questo bombardamento poetico sulla città vuole lanciare in tutto
il mondo il Manifesto di Genova della Rivoluzione Poetica

Lawrence Ferlinghetti
is at the controls of a helicopter
and is swooping dangerously
over the Doge's Palace.
The helicopter dislodges a statue
and soars up towards the one accommodating cloud.
It hovers and feigns
and then it turns to pepper the city of Genoa
with incantatory poems.
The Carabinieri take a few disparate shots
and you can see Ferlinghetti
shaking his fist,
preparing to drop a particularly lethal dose
of André Breton.
The Genoese scatter and duck
and hurry towards the underground
which hasn't been built.
The alleyways of the old quarter
are laced with poems
which wind their unchallengeable way back
to Walt Whitman.
You can see Ferlinghetti clearly now
dapper in his blue shirt.
He's caressing the sexual organs of the city.

When Refusal to do the Shopping
Might be a Criminal Offence

The shopping list crackled on the kitchen table.
I can't possibly buy that, I said. We haven't got the money.
The woman who'd shared my bed for fifteen years
crumpled the list into a ball and shoved it down my neck.

Porco Dio! Porco Dio! Go shop!
I removed the lump now burning into my neck
and dropped it on the floor. I won't.

I heard her jabbing at the phone and chanting
One hundred and twelve
                                            One hundred and twelve.

I listened to the outline of her case:
my English husband refuses to do the shopping.
Refuses to bring baskets of Mediterranean fruit to the marital table.
Refuses to drape cured hams over white plates.
Refuses to glorify the pasta with walnut sauce.
Simply refuses, fucking refuses!
There was a long tearful silence.
Yes, yes, weren't you listening? I told you he was English, inglese.

I slumped into the sofa and listened to my life
breaking into pieces.
I was humming Wither, wither will you flee?
I started watching the Italian version
of Who Wants to be a Millionaire.

I changed my shirt and lit my wife's last cigarette.
Sometime later there was a knock at the door.

I opened it and found a man in uniform
holding two bulging bags from Super Sconto.
His pistol visible, his Puglian face sweating.

When he put the bags down he saluted.

Every cherry pip you spat at me that night
made a pattern on the kitchen floor.
When you went in search of that baby-sweet after dinner cigarette
I said, The policeman smoked it on his way out.

Drowned City
November 2002

What struck me most
about the drowned city
was the way in which
a whole generation of umbrellas
was wiped out.

Some were shoved
cruelly into litter boxes.
Many just drifted around
like tramps, *barboni*,
giving us the questionable benefit
of their death-rattle.

The unequivocally dead
lay on broken backs,
their thin bones
showing signs
of torture.

Jasmine

I got myself to the end of the train
and watched the tracks curve along the coast:
Camogli, Recco, Sori, Nervi.
A collector's set of silver knives.

Summertime, the windows open:
I watched the rocks fragment along the coast.
I watched the vanishing tunnels vanish.
White petals drifted across the tracks.

I've always wanted to travel like this:
watching last things from the end of a train.
The train rocking against the coast like love.
The sea not glass but a carpet of sleep.

I lay down in the drugged aisles
battered by wind and blue curtains
which flapped and flapped and flapped.
I almost relaxed, waiting for the train to break into the city.

City of Malefic Angels
L'amour passe de la ...

for Jack and William

City of my several corpses
City of light summery Italian Waltzes
City of rhyme, city of slime
City of lifts, funiculars and strange particulars
City of Caproni and all that baloney
City of my broken knee
City located precariously on the curve of the sea
City of couplets, triplets and terminations
City of trains and city of rats sliding lasciviously out of drains
City of myopia and dystopia
City of coffee and an interesting variant of English toffee
City of caserme piene di sperma
City of the mind gone wrong, De André, city of song
City of revisionist historians and, increasingly, city of Ecuadorians
City of loose ends and long-toothed friends
City of Rina, I wish I'd seen her one more time
City of ubiquitous vowels, city of inefficient bowels
City of Economia and city of a home-grown version of the *Oresteia*
City of Via Gramsci and my estranged wife the banshee
City of the ghetto, William, Jack and Castelletto
City of Sampdoria and permanently deferred euphoria
City of Crema per il Corpo al Profumo di Patchouli
City of Loredana, Maristela, Gloria and that Scottish girl Julie
City of Valéry, Dickens, Montale, Melville and Hardy
City of green sauce and city of my expensive and not yet completed
  divorce.

Sampierdarena, 1990

for Jack

Do you remember the night you were born?
Rosalba was our gynaecologist of choice.
She smoked incessantly, a flickering of ash
transforming the consulting room
into a not unreasonable display of pointillismo.

Her babies were born in a fix of nicotine.
A gynaecologist who smoked was bound to do well
in those heady day when smoking was almost a necessity.
But a gynaecologist who smoked
and who was blessed with an eye that twitched?
You were born in the hospital of Sampierdarena
in the early hours of March the sixth, 1990.
You were crowned in the sweetness of placenta
and little daubs of excrement.
Rosalba was nimble, her cigarette, her twitching eye,
that pulling of you into the world.

Your mother was led away to recover
and Rosalba said Hold him! Hold him!
We walked, startled father, startled son
along the hospital's marble corridors
edging away from Rosalba's one good eye.
I knew there was a bar across the road
and I put you into my coat pocket like a kilo of trofie
and we slipped into the world of senses.
In the morning I could see mimosa everywhere
and I drank coffee laced with grappa.
Little flakes of brioche landed on your head.
Jack, how many days did we hang out in Bar Franco?

Do you recognise the child? Rosalba asked a little strangely.
Do you know I have seen him somewhere.
I've seen him in the breaking dawn of Castelletto
I've seen him in the labyrinth of the city
I've him in the Bar of Mirrors
I've seen him on the train to Casella
I've seen him in Forte Castellaccio
I've seen him swimming in the waters of Sori.

Blue Towel

I hang a blue towel on the line beneath the window
then I walk around the flat un a melancholic daze.
When I go for the towel a little later
I see it's fallen and snagged on the line below.

Next day I'm staring out of the window
watching a girl taking her pants from the clothesline.
I don't suppose you've come across a blue towel.
Sure, she says, pop down sometime carissimo.
Early evening I'm pushing at her bell.
She opens the door and there's a blue towel
wrapped around her head.

I'm asked if I would like a little grappa
and soon there's a clink of glasses behind the curtain.
I'm looking at the room which consists almost entirely of a bed
which is not unreasonable given her line of work
and several books
including a copy of *Chameleon Tunes*.

She brings a tray with three glasses, one of which is full of ice.
Do you like Billie Holiday? I must have nodded
because we sat there listening to some strange fruit

                             hanging from the trees
sipping chilled grappa
her head wrapped so beautifully in my blue towel.

La Bomba Ratzinger
New Year's Eve, 2005, Recco

We have eaten a pig's foot and large bowl of lentils.
Sarah has opened a bottle of spumante.

Pope Benedict streaks across the sky
followed in his wake by a host of luminaries
cardinals, mystics, unrepentant heretics . . .

Questo é divertente. Che bello! Che bello!
La Bomba Ratzinger! Buon Anno! Buon Anno!

AUGURI! AUGURI!

do help yourself to a little more of the pig.

from Rina's War (2001)

Six

Vapours from Trebor
sweeten the Chesterfield air
and break across the borough's twisted spine.
These travels in a fateful aether.

This was the gateway to heaven
where knee-chapped, hysterical and thin
we boarded the school train.
Ten-year-old wide boys with *Number Six*.
Then – holidays over – we came gently back
with sherbet and love chants.

Bawdsey
1917

There would have been a morning like this.
The house on the edge of the sea
and the waves instructed to be furious.
There would have been maids thrashing
cushions and preparing for the visit.
The butler would insist on being lame.

There would be gulls liberated by the wind
soaring above the punished trees
and the rain would scatter across the lawns.
There would be a fire reticent with its flames
and footsteps bringing a silver tray
to a man in the library who carried a revolver.
News from France.

There would be something like courtesy
and the perfume of leather and the gardener soaked
speaking sotto voce to the trees.
A horse would bolt and the cook would weep.

Sottoripa
1984

I wanted the meanest zone
in the city, so I took a room
in the Sottoripa and lived
with a Persian for six heady months.
He fed me on pistachio nuts
the only thing mamma knew how to send
and boasted about his muscles.

Breakfast was a trip downstairs
coffee followed by grappa followed by coffee
a room full of lined stomachs,
the small fry of the criminal class.
There was much talk about nothing
and life was full of throat-cutting gestures.

If you wanted sex you had to pay for it
or wait until the smallest hours.
The Moroccans were happy to oblige.
Meanwhile the ships drifted
into port to unload their human cargo
and the dogs in the Sottoripa multiplied.

Shutters

Close the shutters, open the shutters, arrange the shutters.
We were delighted with the ritual of our green Genoese shutters.
We studied the relationship between light and shutters.
The room became a fantasy.
Here come Rina and Bruno afraid of the sun.
Let's close the shutters, let us have parcels of light.

Gorleri in Eight Parts

I

1992

I watch the land falling
down to the sea.
The priest died a long time ago
but he still knows how to sing the mass,
still knows how to please God.
The fires that burn across the valleys
are strange communications
and we gather together the scent
of burning wood for an early breakfast.

They built the motorway
to glorify death and
the distant roar of the traffic
makes the crickets leap and leap –
but does not stay the strawberry
grape which buries us, does not
run through our damp cellar,
does not drag us into the light.

2

Each village is built like a fort
to have a wide view of the sea.
Each village self-contained
with a spire to lift the eyes.
Olives provide a living.

Men smoke in the piazza.

On market days the long walk
to sell food, gossip.
Weary feet bathed in the sea.
Urchins swim to the rocks.
Carved niches provide homes
for the Virgin Mothers of God.
Their blue flowers fading.

When the storm comes, panic
The dogs jitter like the possessed.
First we batten down the shutters.
Then we cower in our beds.
The children sleep across our knees.
Sometimes comfort, sometimes tears.
Tomorrow the sun will surge.
The air sweetened with basilico.

3

I dreamed
I was in the piazza of Gorleri.

Old Mama Rina
walked into the sunlight.

She sat on her favourite stone
and started the lamentations.

There were bazookas and rockets.

They were carrying Saint Nicolà
the village protector.

The dead priest led the procession.
He was daubed in splendour.

It was a miracle, a Festa.

4

The blue church of Gorleri.

They hired an ecclesiastical artist
who sprayed the inner walls celeste.
That was, according to the brochure,
between 1863–1887.

The artist – it would seem – in no rush.

The church façade's a slab of pastry.
Dogs pant. Campanile perfection.

You'll have to imagine the celeste.
The doors are always locked,
unless you catch the priest,
who's dead.

5

Surprised by their age
the uncles took out
the battered Fiat
and drove to the hills
to see the baby

Jeck! Jack!

Their movements across the piazza slow.
Zia Sverina with her stick and myopia.
Zio Nirlo with the cough which would carry him off.

6

Il gatto

Leaves of bougainvillea
blow through the streets
and a skeletal cat
is playing with a ghost.

*(Via Badoino Quntilio, an Alpine soldier lost on the Russian Front.
Formerly: 'The Way of the Broken Houses')*

1998

Came Badoino's extremely old sister.
Came Clemé with figs.
Came Rina with lamentations.
Came Bruno with scissors.
Came Enzo with motorino.
Came Signora Maiocchi, first time
out of the house for twenty years.
Came the Englishwoman
from out of her golden cage.
Came the Mayor, spit, spit.
Came the priest, always the priest.
& the band made up for the occasion
rusty but trumpeting.
All coming, all shouting
      Badoino! Badoino!

8

Susanna is walking down to the piazza
and I'm holding a bucket of sheets.
Stai facendo la biancheria? Come sei bravo!
I unlock the gate and climb to Marilena's
whose terrace looks over the roofs of the village.
I drape the white sheets over the railings
and look across the valley.
It's as if someone's given me the world.

Rina's War

Lombardy '43. Fog lingers with fog
and the quiet progress of bicycles
has swallowed the wail of sirens.

Rina cannot see the Germans
and the Germans cannot see Rina.
All lost in the perfection of fog.

Just as the blind can hear the light
Rina cycles through the rice fields
aware of the butcher, the baker,

the priest, the collaborator, their
silent vehicles swishing past
under the shadow of their breath.

At the end of the fog more fog
and a landscape of ghostly bicycles
all ducking and weaving, all hoping.

Octopus

We were two young people
in a hot city
making baby under the blue sky.

You were down at the fish market
gathering an octopus
which you scrubbed and cooked.
I had to eat,
the octopus dripping off my chin.

Oh baby, baby . . .

Ballo

Enzo has ducked down with the grass cutter.
Izio, the electrician, has gone Hawaiian.
Marilena, rich with houses, has beautiful hair.

The lady from Milan doesn't like negri.
She likes the strange vacuum of August
and she believes in the power of prayer.

Susanna in Venice since '68 –
Her son is dancing with the thin blonde girlfriend.
Man spricht Deutsch auf der Piazza.

The old men are smoking like Turks
and forever shouting, Pino's hawking his Olivetti.
No space for hiatus in dialect.

The black shirt is gangly with cropped hair.
He is wearing braces with the faces of the Duce.
He is teaching his son how to tango.

My wife is ladling out sangria
and taking money for the ballo, *ah the ballo!*
Clemé's spilling figs from her pockets.

And there's Bruno the rabbit catcher,
the barber, the olive-bottler,
the voyager, gerontion ball breaker . . .

My wife is dancing with Izio
gliding round and round and round the ballo.
I'm watching his hand on her arse.

After the ballo we stack the chairs,
take a car to the sea; we strip and swim.
And because it is dark we are laughing.

St Anna's Funicular

When I go down to hell
I will take Saint Anna's Funicular.
It will be waiting for me
in the nearly dark of a
velvet-skied Genoese evening.

I will be the only passenger
and the doors will slide shut
with a sublime finality.
It will be quite an occasion,
this journey into eternity.

And in that narrow steep descent
I will be given my last vision
of the city against the sea
and I will pass lighted windows
full of comfort and chandeliers.

Acknowledgements

New poems have appeared in *AN Editions*, *Bad Lilies*, *The Dark Horse*, *The Spectator* and *Wild Court*. Thanks to a great many editors and publishers who have brought out my work over the years, not least *Exacting Clam* (USA) in these more recent times. And thanks to my many friends, poet friends and family. A special thanks to the Bogliasco Foundation, Canneto Editore (Genoa), Massimo Bacigalupo, Guglielmo Trupia who made the film poem *Sottoripa* (https://bit.ly/3UPcQmV), Charles Boyle, Hugo Williams, Christopher Reid and Christopher Hamilton-Emery. I remember Fleur Adcock with a great deal of fondness. I first met her in 1982; she passed away in 2024. She encouraged my writing from the beginning.

This book has been typeset by
SALT PUBLISHING LIMITED
using Sabon, a font designed by Jan Tschichold
for the D. Stempel AG, Linotype and Monotype
Foundries. It has been manufactured using Holmen
Book Cream 65gsm paper, and printed and bound by
Clays Limited in Bungay, Suffolk, Great Britain.

CROMER
GREAT BRITAIN
MMXXV